STEVE
AFGHAN
HEAT

SAS OPERATIONS IN AFGHANISTAN

Dedicated to all the members of the military that have fought in
Afghanistan

Published by Digital Dreams Publishing 2015

Copy editing by Rachel Hunter

ISBN-13: 978-1517202583

ISBN-10: 1517202582

Contents

Foreword

Time and again the SAS have displayed a range of skills and levels of personal courage that have not only made them the envy of the world, but they have also delivered spectacular results. From their inception in the SAS they have been on operations from the Jungles in Belize to Northern Island and the Middle East in Iran and Iraq as well as plenty of other exotic locations. Afghan Heat follows the SAS in Afghanistan giving an intimate picture of what it is like fighting a war hardened enemy in a harsh environment.

The SAS was part of a coalition dismantling, in what US General David Petraeus, the former NATO commander, has described as "an industrial-strength insurgency". The SASs skills have been in almost constant demand since 2001. When two squadrons deployed to Afghanistan under 'Operation Enduring Freedom' to overthrow the Taliban, as part of the war on terror. During the early years of their involvement in the war on terror, they were badly under-resourced.

This book is based on real operations, with the fast paced action being both gritty and graphical at times, as the SAS battle against overwhelming odds in a hostile land. Fighting a war hardened enemy with years of experience fighting occupying forces. Even these elite soldiers with advanced weaponry and immense fire support at their disposal are put to the ultimate test of skill and courage, fighting in the 'Stan.' The story cuts out the hours spent waiting for an operation or something to 'kick off.' The phrase 'train hard and fight easy' is a cornerstone of the SAS and the British Army doctrine. Over preparation is a gift in an ideal world, although operationally that is not always the case. Intelligence can change by the minute, a firefight can change in seconds. All these are things that the SAS trains and prepares for, even if improvisation is all that you have left in a tactical situation. Something the SAS have become adept at over its long and colourful history. For every 10 minutes of action there are several more hours of boredom waiting or watching in an observation post, or holed up in one of the many bases scattered throughout Afghanistan preparing for the next operation.

The SAS like the rest of the allied forces in Afghanistan have to deal with the horror of war on a daily basis. There are many unsung heroes that we pass by in the street, many of whom are still struggling to deal with the mental as well as physical scars of being at war. For this reason, for every copy of Afghan Heat sold a donation will be made to, "Help for Heroes" which provide support for wounded soldiers.

A man who is good enough to shed his blood for his country is enough to be given a fair deal afterwards.

Theodore Roosevelt
4 July 1903

The SAS is currently involved in operations all over the world. 22 SAS Regiment is the regular full-time regiment and there is also 21 SAS regiment, which is made up of reserve soldiers and 23 SAS which was formed by renaming the Reserve Reconnaissance unit. The regimental headquarters of 22 Special Air Service is based at Stirling Lines on the outskirts of Hereford. It is a modern complex that accommodates the regiment's five squadrons – four "sabre", or fighting, squadrons, plus another relatively new squadron that is used for specialist surveillance operations – as well as Special Forces signals and reconnaissance squadrons. Also units of the recently established Special Forces Support Group (SFSG), which is mainly drawn from the Parachute Regiment.

22 SAS Regiment is made up of four operational squadrons (A, B, D, G) and from 2005 the highly covert E Squadron that work alongside Mi6. Each of these squadrons has about 60 men in them and is commanded by a major. The squadron is then further divided into four troops; each commanded by a captain and consists of 16 men. The smallest denomination is a patrol, which is comprised of four men. Within each Squadron, there are four distinct troops Boat, Mountain, Air and Mobility each having set specialities such as vehicle maintenance, parachuting, scuba diving, and fighting in arctic conditions. The Hereford base is completely self-contained and deliberately keeps its distance from the rest of the Armed Forces. They can call on its own fleet of helicopters as well as specially adapted Hercules transport aircraft that are kept on permanent standby at RAF Brize Norton in Oxfordshire. The regiment, even has its own budget, which it uses to acquire state-of-the-art surveillance and communications equipment, as well as the latest weaponry. Such is its determination to be self-sufficient. The SAS even trains its own German Shepherd tracker dogs, which are parachuted into hostile environments to conduct searches and have proved very effective in Afghanistan.

It was Ahmad Shah Durrani, who unified the Pashtun tribes and in 1747 founded Afghanistan. Afghanistan has served as a buffer between the British and Russian Empires until it finally won independence from notional British control in 1919. A brief experiment in democracy ended with a coup in 1973 and then in 1978 a Communist counter-coup. In 1979, the Soviet Union invaded to support the Afghan Communist regime that was struggling to remain in power. This started off a long and protracted war. Then in 1989, USSR withdrew under relentless pressure by an internationally supported anti-Communist mujahedin rebel force. A series of subsequent civil wars finally saw Kabul fall in 1996 to the Taliban. The Taliban is a hard line Pakistani-sponsored movement that emerged in 1994 to end the country's civil war and anarchy between various factions and bring in a strict Islamic law. Following the terrorist attacks on 11 September 2001, a US, Allied, and anti-Taliban Northern Alliance came together to topple the Taliban for the sheltering of Osama Bin Laden who was subsequently killed by SEAL Team Six on May 2 2011. At the 2001 UN-sponsored Bonn Conference, held to establish a process for political reconstruction in Afghanistan that included the adoption of a new constitution and in 2004 a presidential election followed in 2005 by the National Assembly elections. In December 2004, Hamid Karzai became the first democratically elected president of Afghanistan. The National Assembly was then inaugurated the following December. In August 2009, Karzai was re-elected for a second term. Despite the gains towards building a stable central government, a resurgent Taliban along with continuing provincial instability - particularly in the south and the east - remain a large challenge for the Afghan Government. Allied troops are due to leave in 2014 and hand, full control to the Afghan government.

With a population of around 30,419,928 and religiously made up about 80% Sunni Muslim, 19% Shia Muslim 19%, 1% others. The languages spoken are Afghan Persian or Dari 50%, Pashto 35%, Turkic languages (primarily Uzbek and Turkmen) 11%, and 30 minor languages (primarily Balochi and Pashai) 4%. There is a large amount of bilingualism, however Dari functions as the lingua Franca.

The culture of Afghanistan has been influenced by the surrounding countries and even slightly by the occupying countries over the years. In the southern and eastern region, as well as western Pakistan. Western

Pakistan was historically part of Afghanistan. The Pashtun people live by the Pashtun culture and they follow Pashtunwali (way of the Pashtuns). The western, northern, and central regions of Afghanistan are influenced by neighbouring Central Asian and Persian cultures. Afghans living in the cities, in particular Kabul, are further influenced to some degree by the Indian culture through Bollywood films and music. Some of the non-Pashtuns who live in close proximity with Pashtuns have adopted Pashtunwali in a process called Pashtunization (or Afghanization) while some Pashtuns and others became Persianized.

Afghanistan is a mountainous country completely surrounded by land and shares its borders with Pakistan, Tajikistan, Iran, Turkmenistan, Uzbekistan and China. The Hindu Kush Mountains, which run northeast to southwest across the country, divide it into three major regions. The Central Highlands, which form part of the Himalayas and account for roughly two thirds of the country's area. The Southwestern Plateau, accounts for about 25% of the land. The smaller Northern Plains area has Afghanistan's most fertile area of soil.

British Special Forces operations in southern Afghanistan were centred on persuading mid-ranking Taliban leaders that they were better off working with the Afghan government. This involved a mixture of "hard arrests" — snatch operations to grab key Taliban leaders to gather intelligence — and "offensive action" in which Taliban leaders were killed. These operations were happening every day with a mixture of larger scale operations, hard arrests and offensive actions – all of which is having an impact on the Taliban leadership. The SAS continues to undertake smaller scale operations and aid Afghan Special Forces.

"Sabre" squadrons of SBS and SAS are based at the tactical group headquarters in Kandahar. Unlike Iraq, where the SAS was in the lead,

Afghanistan has seen a dramatic increase in operations by the SBS, which has seen its budget increase from £17m in 2001 to £160m in 2010. During the winter of 2010 the SBS reverted to arctic warfare skills, using skis to track down Taliban commanders above the snowline in the Hindu Kush.

Along with the SAS, there was the Australian SAS, Delta Force and the US Navy SEAL's amongst other Special Forces operating in Afghanistan. They too have undertaken some amazing operations. One worthy of mention is the Australian SAS battle at Eastern Shah Wali Kot covered later on in the book. There is also the rescue of Helen Johnston in 2012 by the SAS and Delta Force as a combined operation.

The SAS has fought a hard war, along with the rest of the armed forces out in Afghanistan. Afghanistan is a hostile environment fraught with danger – extreme temperatures along with a battle hardened enemy - with the ability to fight hard and deal some devastating blows to allied forces. The sheer scale of Afghanistan has meant it has been hard to rid the country of Taliban forces. More often than not they move their bases of operations around Afghanistan, even just into the border of Pakistan, using fringe villages along the boarders as safe havens to train and prepare for battle. They observe us as much as we observe them, trying to understand our tactics and doctrine. They are an enemy not to be underestimated, nor is the hatred that many have for anything western. Even their own countrymen who have more tolerant views on Islam, become targets if they will not follow the Taliban way of life and beliefs. Afghanistan is part of a wider war on extremists, who want to force their particular way of life or beliefs onto a country. There are still many unstable countries – some fighting their own civil wars, with groups of extremists waiting in the wings to gain power. I am not religious in any way, but from what I have seen, tolerance and understanding are what many of these extremists lack.

They are blinkered by their own beliefs to the point, that they believe what they are doing is somehow holy and right. In their eyes, they believe what they are doing will lead to a better world. These extremists will stop at nothing to challenge democracy as the recent events in Paris, France has shown. The war in Afghanistan is far from over the Afghan people and the Government are still battling the Taliban. The risk from extremists to global security has never been higher.

Prologue

Lying down in the prone position and feeling the warmth of the hot ground beneath me - C8 Carbine at the ready. My senses heightened and in a state of alert - I reflected on being an SAS operative, the glow of pride swelled from within. I was an elite soldier in one of the best regiments in the world. I had worked hard to get here and even harder to stay in the Regiment. The SAS take the best of the best, they don't just need excellent soldiers, but soldiers who can work as a cohesive team and be able to make decisions under stressful conditions.

I had been laying on the sun baked and dusty soil for the past three hours, waiting for the order to go. All I had to look at from the vegetation I was hiding in, was a few trees and thorny bushes surrounding a freshly ploughed field. There was nothing to be heard, but the odd rustle from the surrounding trees, as the slightly warm breeze wafted over me giving a little relief from the heat. Lying in wait had given me plenty of thinking time, maybe too much. During my time in the regiment, over thinking is nearly as bad as not thinking at all. We had been on 'hard routine' for the past three days and could not wait to get back for a proper shit, shower and shave, followed by a cooked meal. There was only so many 'rat packs' army speak for rations, you could endure. Although I did quite like burgers and beans followed by the chocolate pudding. Hard routine means taking everything you need with you and everything back including our own defecation in plastic bags. I personally love being out in the field, I hate being stuck on base, especially so when I was in the Para's and we were give shit cleaning jobs just to fill the time.

The operation today was to seize a Taliban leader from his compound in Farah; normally this would have been carried out at night. However, the intelligence had placed him staying at the compound and likely to leave before dusk. Intelligence had it only lightly defended – but we distrusted intelligence nearly as much as the actual Taliban. It was supposed to be only lightly defended and the opportunity to 'get him' was considered too good to miss. Farah is located in the Western part of Afghanistan near to Iran. It is one of the thirty-four provinces of Afghanistan. One of a series of citadels built by Alexander the Great is located in Farah. Our objective was right on the fringe of Farah, in one of the hundreds of villages in the area. One thing you are not truly aware about Afghanistan until you are actually in Afghanistan, is the sheer size of the country. Farah for instance, is half the size of South Korea. In parts of Farah, the area is semi-arid with almost desert like conditions as you head towards the mountains in the North East. The rest of the area is a patchwork of crop fields and dusty tracks, with only the odd main road that lead in and out of Farah itself.

It was an isolated compound just outside a village that we would assault. A compound is just a low mud building, which is usually built in a square with a central open area and rooms around the perimeter. The walls are quite thick and is a heavy duty structure that can take some pounding from small arms fire. A single 500lb bomb dropped from above would obliterate most compounds in one go.

Eight of us in total were to carry out a daytime assault and grab the target before any reinforcements could be sent. The target was a high-ranking Taliban intelligence officer. The Taliban in the area did have a couple of 5th generation Toyota Hilux's that had RPGs and high calibre machine guns mounted on them. The high calibre machine gun alone could tear us to shreds. These Hilux's were really a job for an Apache to deal with - our C8's had little chance against them, less a lucky shot or a large amount of lead. With us all only carrying 240 rounds each, we did not have the ammunition to waste either. Along with the C8, I was also carrying Sig

Sauer P226 handgun as my sidearm or secondary weapon. The P226 is a German manufactured 9mm pistol capable of carrying up to 20 9mm rounds. The company is of Swiss origin, but due to Swiss export laws on firearms. The P226 had to be manufactured and exported outside of Switzerland. The US Navy SEALs have used the P226 since the mid-1980s. They have their own version with a stainless steel slide engraved with an anchor to designate them as Navy Special Ops pistols. The word is the P226 will soon be replaced by the Glock 17 Gen 4, introduced in 2010, a polymer-framed, short recoil operated pistol.

With final prep completed, C8 made ready, safety catch set to single shot and its butt in my shoulder. We moved off, the best way in was via a wadi then making use of some dead ground, before running the final short distance to the compound. If we came into contact it would be a case of pushing forward unless it was too intense, then it would be about putting the maximum amount of fire down and getting the hell out of there as per op orders. Higgs and the rest of the patrol had the mentality, fuck the op orders, we never go back only forwards. The hot sun beat down on us - if I was not wearing gloves my rifle would have been too hot to hold. Sweat trickled down the side of my face and onto my neck. The wadi offered a decent level of protection even if we all kicked up small clouds of dust with every step as we dodged round larger rocks and boulders. When you begin an assault, it is amazing how your situational awareness kicks in, almost as if you have the sight and hearing ability of an Owl. Even the slightest noise or movement makes you flick your head left or right, moving your weapon to follow your eyes covering your arcs. The rest of the lads were all alert and professional like an SAS switch had been flicked on. Only a few hours earlier they had filled an officer's boot with shaving foam and filled the cups of sugar with salt next to the Burco in the ops room. This school boy type behaviour was all part of the coping mechanism – dealing with death on a daily basis in a hostile country takes its toll, even on highly trained and resilient SAS troopers. In war people lose their lives, even though we are deployed to try and protect people. That is how I justify what I do – that I am here to protect innocent people from being drawn into wars or suffer at the hands of terrorists.

Within minutes, we were only a few hundred metres away from our objective and slowed our pace and movement right down – making best use of any available cover as we darted across any open ground. It must have worked as we made it to the compound without being spotted. Four of us in one patrol huddled up by the front entrance to the compound as the other patrol went round to the rear. The idea was for the four of us to burst in through the front and then the patrol at the rear catch any fleeing Taliban – which was likely to contain our target as well. It was a tactic we had used several times before to good effect.

I could feel my heart almost thumping in my throat and to this day, I still get a bout of diarrhoea before every operation. Maybe my nerves get the better of me. The strange part is that when in the heat of battle I stay as steady as a rock and just get on with the job at hand, even with bullets impacting the ground inches away from me. My training kicks in and I go about my job as if in automatic pilot, instinctively carrying out my skills and drills. That is the real key to good soldiering - doing something enough times in training that it becomes instinctive. So in the heat of battle you don't have to think about clearing a stoppage or changing a magazine, all your focus is on finding a target and putting it down.

We gave the other patrol, exactly two minutes to get into position before we were to begin the assault. The two minutes passed, we made our way into the compound – literally bursting through the door and almost knocking the door off the hinges. After Higgs gave the door an almighty kick with his size 13 boots. Some shouts in Pashto could be heard within seconds of us bursting through the door, followed by some ineffective rifle fire. The rounds bounced off the wall to the far left of us. Higgs to my left spotted where the fire was coming from – he let off two rounds in quick succession and they found their target. The Taliban fighter slumped to the floor, dropping his AK-47 with a loud clang onto the hard stone floor of the compound. Make no doubt, the AK-47 is a powerful rifle, its rounds can go through a brick wall like a knife through butter at close to medium range. Even hiding behind a wall gives you no guarantee a bullet will not make its way through, after a few rounds have been fired on the same area.

We pushed forward and I scanned the sparse room for any more surprises, by now the other Taliban occupying the compound had fled towards the rear. As they got to the rear I could hear more shouting in both Pashto and English, as the other patrol team grabbed the fleeing Taliban as they tried to escape. I could hear the lads shouting and grunting trying to control the Taliban fighters - who had no intention of coming quietly. As the other team got each one under control and cuffed them, they threw them up against the wall, before removing their weapons and carrying out a full body search. The trouble with a hard arrest, even with speed and force, you have no idea if they have some form of suicide vest strapped to them. Speed and surprise with quickly cuffing to the rear with cable ties before a thorough search. Most of us would much rather slot them through the head than give them a chance to take us all out with a suicide vest.

The speed at which the Taliban fighters had decided to flee out the back got me and the rest of the patrol a little concerned. The Taliban - masters of booby traps and IEDs (Improvised Explosive Device) through years of practice under the Russian occupation. Even now, they were getting more

16

and more sophisticated by the day. We decided to stand firm and wait until it had been confirmed that the intended target had been captured. Kneeling down and constantly scanning for any surprises.

The minutes passed and Higgs grew restless – he decided to make a move. I let Higgs get about 5 metres in front before following him. I then made it another couple of metres before I felt an intense heat on my face followed by a pressure wave. That pressure wave sent me back further than I had come forward, before I finally hit the hard stone floor almost horizontal. I was unable to breath for a few seconds and had an intense buzzing in my ears. As I sat up, I realised what had happened, Higgs had set off some form of IED. What was left of Higgs was splatted all over the wall of the rear room in the compound - with a large chunk of torso lying in a large pool of blood. The sickening smell of flesh and explosive cordite smell, filled the compound after the initial smoke from the explosion had cleared. The best comparison I can give is the smell of burnt burgers mixed with the smell of fireworks on bonfire night.

An IED is basically a homemade bomb constructed and then deployed in more guerrilla type tactics, they are also known as roadside bombs. They can be constructed of conventional military explosives, such as an artillery round which is then attached to a detonating mechanism. The explosives can even be homemade and they are getting more and more sophisticated all the time, although they are often unstable and prone to explode without warning. Sometimes the instability is from the explosives used or just the poor construction of the detonator.

In the second Iraq War, IEDs were used extensively against US-led Coalition forces and by the end of 2007 they had become responsible for approximately 63% of Coalition deaths in Iraq. In Afghanistan they have been used to good effect and have caused over 66% of the Coalition casualties in the Afghanistan War.

The patrol members at the back of the compound had their hands full trying to control the prisoners, even though they had been cuffed with plastic ties. Time was of the essence and we needed to get out quickly. I pulled a body bag out and with Knight, we began the grim task of scooping up as much as we could of Higgs's body. There was no time to pick up all the individual pieces just the larger chunks of flesh and what was left of Higgs caved in head - which was now a bloody and tangled mass of hair, teeth and flesh. It was probably the hardest and most gruesome thing I have ever had to do – still in shock and feeling dazed from the explosion. The sight of Higgs remains splatted around a kitchen is etched into my memory and nightmares to this very day.

Higgs was a 6 foot 4 man mountain and a person you would not want to mess with, just by looking at him, his size made him almost unusable for 'blending in' type operations. Looks were deceiving as the minute he opened his mouth, he could have you in stitches. Higgs was originally from Manchester and one of a small number who had come via a unit other than the Para's. He had served for five years with the Mercian's and risen to Corporal, before passing SAS selection on his second attempt. He lived to fight and he was truly in love with his weapon called Betty, after Betty Boop whom he had always said was a rather animated character. His jokes were nearly as bad as the toxic gas that he could release from his arse, and after three days in an OP with him, you cried out for fresh air. His life was the Army, with no plans for life after the 'Regiment.' I guess, is he would of gone on to be some form of mercenary fighting someone else's war just for the thrill of the fight. An adrenaline junkie with guns is a good way to sum Higgs up. Patriotic to the end and loved his country, even if he was a Manchester City fan, but we all have things we are not proud of...

It was not too far from the Compound to our extraction point across a couple of fields, although using as much cover as possible from clumps of trees and dead ground. A Chinook was due in about 30 minutes – we would need to move quickly in order to make it. It was a silent fast-paced walk back to the extraction point, other than the Taliban chirping up in Pashto. Our thoughts were all on Higgs – why had he decided to take such a risk on an op that had ran so smoothly? We had already got the target without as much as a scratch on any one of us. Our patrol leader summed it up, "Higgs you're a right stupid fucker." We would all miss him along with his bad jokes and banter. This is war and in war people die, and if you dwell too much you would never be able to carry on with your job.

On the flight back to base with what was left of Higgs in a bag at my feet, I just stared at the half-empty body bag for the whole of the flight back to Kandahar. I never saw anything of the tracer fire or the RPG that had missed us by inches as we flew back to base. All I knew was that I had lost a good friend and colleague - he was not the first and would certainly not be the last...

Chapter One – In the Beginning

David Stirling originally founded the SAS in 1941, during the Western Desert Campaign of the Second World War. After the war the SAS were disbanded only to be reformed as the 21 SAS Territorial Army regiment, which then led to the formation of the regular army 22 SAS Regiment in 1952. The SAS has come a long way from its early days in Hereford in the 1960s, when the regiment was regarded by the military establishment as a dare-devil bunch of cutthroats, only to be used in the most extreme circumstances. The SAS has become a highly professional body of men and renowned the World over. To be able to wear that beige beret complete with the dagger with, "who dares wins" insignia is something many soldiers yearn for. Even though the failure rate during selection is around 90% and you only get two attempts to pass selection.

I found being a soldier has come strangely naturally to me; it was not something I had ever really thought about doing. Certainly not something I would have been any good at doing. My earliest memories are playing in the brick room at nursery and getting a train set at Christmas not long after my December birthday. I cannot say I really got on well at primary school. I seemed to spend far too much time in the naughty corner. I cannot say I disliked school, just as I cannot say I liked school. I suppose it was not too bad, I loved playing Army round a grassy mound at the edge of the playground. Possibly it was a precursor for my future employment? From primary school, I moved into a decent enough secondary school. I was not a natural academic and found school a difficult place. I was, however, quite good at rugby and swimming even though I would not class myself as the sporty type. I think being quite skinny, helped me to run quite fast due to the lack of weight I had to carry around, I would later find that an advantage in the Army, becoming one of so called 'racing snake's'. I don't think I would have done quite as well at school, but for my parents cajoling me along. Having both a mum and dad who were teachers, meant they took education seriously, when I did not. I got thrown out of German and sent to do extra PE after just one lesson. What I was good at though, was art and modular technology. My maths was quite good, but English was none too great - even as I write this book - I am sure many will have every right to criticise my grammar or writing style along with being the original Walter Mitty. Which, interestingly, recently became a movie with Ben Stiller playing Walter. No idea why they did not ask my good self to play the lead?

During my second year of GCSEs I got my first proper job after a paper round, working at Burger King. I was on what was called production, making the burgers or sandwich as they are called, by the end of a shift you ended up smelling like a burger with very greasy hair. I could only take 8 months of that job before packing it in and looking for new employment. I managed to pick up a summer job at my local garden centre. Most of my time was spent with my new girlfriend who was the reason I stayed on in the sixth form and did not go to college to do a BTEC, which would have suited me much better with no exams! I maybe would have got a little less distracted as well...

I then managed to scrape one A level at grade E and fail another two with a U. It was partly though my own laziness and partly due to the break up with my girlfriend of two years, in the middle of my exams. After I got my results, university was out of the question unless I did some retakes. I had had enough of education and just wanted to get a job. I applied and got a full-time job in a Hi-Fi shop after having had an interest in Hi-Fi equipment for a number of years.

After two years working in a Hi-Fi shop that was slowly driving me mad with boredom, I was desperate to find something that was more of a challenge. I had originally wanted to be a firefighter, and had applied twice and twice failed the aptitude test, twice on the maths element. I knew I needed to find a career or job that gave me some excitement. I really was not the office type, the thought of sitting at a desk day after day horrified me.

Wandering the bustling city centre streets at lunchtime, I wandered past the Amy careers office and a poster caught my eye. It was the adventure bit that had made me think along with the picture of a tank. I carried on walking and did not think anything more of it. Two weeks later, I got the sack from my job and deserved the sack to be honest. Too lazy to go and get some money out of the cashpoint. I opened the till and took 20p out to give me enough money for a snickers bar. I had every intention of replacing it at lunch. Unbeknown my manager was behind me dealing with a customer and saw what I had just done. Theft is theft no matter what the amount is, or my later intentions. He had no choice but to sack me on the spot and I cannot blame him I had been a total dickhead.

Out of work, I was in need of a new job, and that is when my thoughts turned back to the Army careers centre. The same day I was sacked, I went down to the Army careers centre and had a chat with a recruitment advisor and picked up some glossy brochures and booked an appointment to sit my British Army Recruit Battery (BARB) test. My BARB test results came back as quite high and the one of the officers asked had I thought about becoming an officer. I remember the recruiting sergeant and officer having an argument, about what would be best for me to do. I had a high enough score to undertake a more technical trade. But I wanted to be where the action was on the frontline and I was looking towards joining a Tank

Regiment. I don't know why but the thought of driving a tank was quite appealing.

I went through the recruiting process including the two-day selection process at an Army Development and Selection Centre. Where, I went through a range of strength and stamina tests, as well as a 1.5-mile run. It was after my results came through, that suggested my physical fitness lent itself to becoming a Para. At the time, the thought of jumping out of a perfectly flyable plane held no real pleasure whatsoever. However, the kudos of being a more elite soldier got the better of me and off I went for the 3day Parachute Regiment Assessment Centre (PRAC) at Catterick, which I passed.

Maybe it was good that I had not been let loose with a tank, as the only time I tried to drive a tank, was at the REME (Royal Electrical Mechanical Engineers) training centre in Bordon. I managed to get the tank I was driving, stuck in a ditch on the course and threw its track. The best part was it was a recovery tank that now needed to be recovered by an Army bulldozer.

Two months later, I was starting my training as a Para at Catterick. The initial training was the standard infantry soldier training of the Combined Infantry Course (CIC) called the PARA Combat Infantryman's Course.

"The Combat Infantryman's Course – PARA builds up recruits' skills and fitness bit by bit. In rough order, this involves learning individual skills first, followed by team/section skills and then platoon skills, ending with an assessment.

During training, recruits are taught the importance of discipline, integrity, loyalty and respect for others. They learn that being a soldier is about putting others first and having the courage to do the right thing in any given situation.

This version of the CIC is two weeks longer than the Line Infantry version. Greater emphasis is placed on fitness, bearing in mind the high fitness standards of the Parachute Regiment.

Personnel administration

Personal administration means everything to do with looking after self and kit, in the field as well as in camp. The more organised a man is, the easier he will find it to live like a soldier.

Weapons training

Recruits learn how to handle the SA80 rifle, the Light Machine Gun and the General Purpose Machine Gun, as well as how to use night viewing devices. They start on simulators before moving on to ranges and field firing exercises. There's a five-day live firing exercise at the end of the course.

Drill

Drill means military procedures and movements, such as marching and parading. Learning drill makes a soldier disciplined and teaches him to take pride in his appearance and manner.

The Pass Out Parade at the end of training is a public demonstration of these skills.

Fieldcraft

These are the basic skills a soldier needs to work and survive in the field. Areas covered include camouflage and concealment, map reading, observation, first aid and defence measures. Skills are tested in exercises during the course, culminating in a final exercise during Week 23.

Fitness

There's lots of exercise in the course including sports, running, gym work, swimming, the assault course and general physical training.

Fitness is very important. The training is tough, so it's important that recruits get in shape before they arrive at ITC Catterick. The fitter they are, the easier it is. It's vital that recruits don't let their fitness slip between selection and arrival at ITC Catterick. To get fit, and stay that way, we suggest that recruits put an exercise programme together. The programme needs to combine stamina exercises – such as running and swimming – and strength exercises like press-ups. Recruits should spend between 40 and 60 minutes exercising, four days a week. Recruits due to arrive at ITC Catterick will find the Army Fitness site useful – click 'Fitness' on the right.

Teamwork

Adventurous Training is an important part of the course, comprising challenging outdoor activities, such as abseiling, kayaking and rock climbing. All these improve a soldier's teamwork and initiative. And they're great fun too! Soldiers work as a team, so it is important everyone shares the same values."- source British Army Website.

With the initial CIC complete, I then progressed onto the Pegasus Company (P Coy) element of the course that was also partially blended into the later phase of CIC course. All other recruits wanting to gain their Para wings go through the All Arms Pre-Parachute Selection (AAPPS). This course has to be undertaken by any officer or soldier who wishes to join an airborne unit. The training so far had been quite gruelling and challenging. I don't mind admitting I thought about quitting on more than one occasion. The final three weeks of the 23 week course were spent with further live firing exercises and learning to use a variety of weapons systems and even driver training.

"The Paratrooper is required to be physically fit and mentally robust. He has to demonstrate motivation, self-reliance, initiative and

intelligence. Through rigorous selection and hard training the airborne soldier is expected to develop resilience, self-confidence and a fierce determination to succeed, whatever the difficulties. These qualities have proved a winning factor time and again on operations"- source British Army Website.

The Parachute Regiment forms the airborne infantry element of 16 Air Assault Brigade. We can be deployed anywhere in the world and are used to support Special Forces. I joined 1 PARA after two years with 2 PARA who are the SFSG (Special Forces Support Group) and provide specialist infantry support to Special Forces, anywhere in the world. The basic skills required to serve in 1 PARA were those you I had gained in training and during my time in 2 PARA. It was working with the SAS lads and watching the, in action that made me want to become one of them. I knew I needed to do at least three years in the Para's first, which included my first tour of Afghanistan when I was with 2 PARA. Afghanistan was my first taste of death and the first time I had to kill. I never joined up thinking that one day I might have to kill someone.

As a young PARA deployed to Afghanistan, it was not long into my tour that I made my first kill. The heat and the terrain took some getting used to, being in a combat zone I did feel a little jittery. But I had a job to do and by focusing on that, instead of dwelling on the dangers of being in a war zone, I soon settled into the routine. Two weeks into my deployment I had settled in with my platoon at our CP (Command Post). Not the most luxurious of places to be, but it was a reasonably secure compound with a rather pockmarked wall surrounding it, from previous decades of fighting. We had just received orders that we should own the night, which meant more night patrols. Night patrols played havoc with your body clock until you got used to them or got adept at just being able to fall asleep as soon as you got told to rest.

I left our CP at 23:00 hours on a cool, crisp but dark night - we dropped as quietly as possible into the canal that was adjacent our CP. We made our way as quietly as possible through water up to our knees to a crossroads where the Taliban had regularly laid IEDs, which wreaking havoc with convoys getting through. Only two days ago a Mastiff, a six wheel heavily armoured truck had lost a wheel to an IED. Thankfully without any injuries to the crew. We had not lost anyone out of the platoon so far. I hoped it would stay that way for as long as possible.

The plan was to set up a covert observation post overlooking the junction and lie in wait for the IED team to appear. I had been placed in the team armed with a Javalin. Our position was on a compound roof, that we only fought over a few days previously. The idea was to take the IED team out with the Javalin - rather than getting into a running firefight and draw attention to the patrol. The Javelin is a US fire-and-forget missile with automatic guidance. Normally used as an anti-tank weapon, it's also good for what in Army speak is called 'bunker busting' or simply taking out enemy positions. At around £80,000 $123,000, each shot is not cheap - but we had some rounds nearing expiry date that needed to be used. For some reason, I had been trusted with firing the Javalin. I had fired my rifle on quite a few occasions already and as far as I knew, had not made a kill yet.

At five past midnight, we observed two men moving around near to the junction, it was hard to make out what they were doing but it certainly looked like they were digging. The night vision goggles gave a green tinge to the dark night and the men in the distance. What I could make out was two dark silhouettes standing in a field. Everyone now had their eyes trained on these two men. We were all so busy studying these two men we failed to notice a car to our far right moving at a moderate pace towards our position. The two men digging in the field were actually a farmer and his son tending to the wheat fields at a very strange time.

I was ready to fire and was awaiting the order from my section commander. He decided to hold off for a bit longer, for some reason had a gut feeling that this all seemed too easy. Those gut feelings, saved the lives of the farmer and his son, as given the order I would have fired my Javelin directly at them.

The car slowed down as it approached the junction and finally diverted our attention. I got orders to stand down and observe. The car got closer and closer, it was not moving at any great speed and through night vision goggles I was trying to work out if it was more civilians or something more sinister.

As the car pulled up to the junction, the farmer and his son almost seemed to know whom they were and quickly fled. One of the men got out of the car and went into the car boot to retrieve something. He then came back round towards the front of the car carrying a box. Everyone, including myself knew it must be an IED, but our section commander wanted to be sure. We all watched them plant an IED before he decided to give me the order to fire, just in case they turned out to be civilians.

I watched the man go to near the edge of the road and start shifting some dirt with his hands. He was not actually digging, but looking for wires to a pre-planted IED and needed its battery connecting up to make it live. We had only been searched the day before, so had this IED been missed? The man was most almost certainly a Taliban fighter.

My section commander wanted to get both of them and the car if he could. At the current distance between the car and the Taliban fighter attaching a battery to an IED the Javelin may have got both, but he wanted to be certain. As the Taliban fighter got about a metre from the car, I was given the order to fire. With an almighty whoosh pushing me backwards slightly, the Javalin made its way to the car after I had lined it up and ensure the missile had a lock. On impact the HEAT (High-Explosive Anti-Tank) warhead caused a large explosion that lit up the dark night sky, followed by a plume of dark and dirty smoke. This was soon followed, by bits of the car flying up in the air before raining down on the road. It was a confirmed kill, my first kill - what was left of the Taliban fighters lay strewn across the road as a smouldering pile of flesh and car parts. I had no emotion that I had just killed two people, in many ways it was almost surreal and you felt detached. It was like I was sitting on an Xbox playing Call of Duty, just without the smell of explosives and a cool breeze wafting over me.

I really enjoyed being in the army the camaraderie and banter were all par for the course and had numerous jokes including having my eyebrows shaven off once. One of the other elements about being in the Army is than other than Booze and fags you don't really have that much to spend your money on. I don't smoke and as for booze, he one time I drank eight pints in one night, I went yellow for about three days, so to say I was a light weight was an understatement. I was always happy with a couple of pints rather than going until I could stand no longer. Instead, I seemed to blow my money on a whole string of cars, starting off with a Vauxhall Corsa and then Astra Sri, before moving onto various BMW's in saloon and coupe, culminating in an M3. Then going a bit more sensible with various BMW 1 Series including an epic 130i complete with its straight six engine and 255Bhp. I really was a salesperson's dream…

That is one of the shocks when you come out of the Army and have to pay accommodation and food costs, along with all the other delightful bills that only ever seem to go up!

Chapter Two - Selection

After serving in the Para's for four years, I decided to try to pass SAS selection. This would be even harder and much more demanding than P Coy. I trained for weeks and weeks to ensure I was as physically fit as possible. The SAS selection process though, is not just about physical fitness, but mental too. Being able to quell the pain and not through the towel in when the going gets tough – takes a strong mind, a mind, even stronger than I had needed four years previously on my P Coy. Everyone has different opinions about selection, but all I can tell is that it is damned hard. You are pushed to your limits and beyond. You may spend a day lugging Jerry cans of water up and down a hill, get your head down for two hours before being awoken and taken on a long March. They would tantalise you with a truck that would take you away from all the hurt and pain. This is where the strong mental element came in. Being able to overcome the pain and the wish to give up and just keep going. Throughout my training I always took the light hearted demeanour about everything. It was best to just take it on the chin and get on with it. No point moaning and groaning, if something needed to be done. This was exactly one of the elements the SAS was looking for. An individual who would just get stuck in, no matter how hard the task. My biggest Achilles heel was and still is to a point, sleep deprivation. That was a challenge I had to overcome during selection and find ways to keep my mind active, not giving in to the tiredness and fatigue.

The selection course itself was made up of three phases. The first selection phase was the endurance phase. This first phase consisted of fitness and navigation, or 'the hills' stage. This was the endurance portion of selection and was to test not only my physical fitness, but also my mental stamina. To pass this phase, you did require a high level of determination and self-reliance was vital. I was amazed at the number that dropped out during the first week of this phase.

The actual hills stage lasted 3 weeks and took place in the Brecon Beacons and Black Hills of South Wales. You had to carry an ever-increasingly-heavy bergan over a series of long timed hikes, navigating between checkpoints. No encouragement or criticism was provided by the supervising staff at the checkpoints which had to be reached within set time limits. If you did not quite make a timing you were given a 'gypsy warning' you could only get one of those or it was off to platform four. Platform four was were you took the train to take you home having failed selection. The SAS Directing Staff (DS) were all fully-badged members of the regiment and just observed, leaving all of us to our own devices. This was a marked contrast from my experience in the Para's. There we would have instructors shouting constant instructions at us, along with encouragement and abuse.

The endurance phase culminated with what is called, "The long drag," which a 40-mile trek is carrying a 55lb bergan that must be completed in under 24 hours.

On completion of the Endurance Phase and with over 50% of the original candidates, RTU'd (Returned To Unit) we began the next phase Jungle Training. This training takes place in Belize, in the heart of deep jungles. Here we learnt the basics of surviving and patrolling in the harsh conditions. SAS jungle patrols have to live for weeks behind enemy lines, in four man patrols, living on rations. Jungle training weeded out those who couldn't handle the discipline required to keep themselves and their kit in good condition whilst on long range patrol in difficult conditions.

Again, there was a mental component being tested, not just a physical. As Special Forces need men who can work under relentless pressure, in horrendous environments for weeks on end, without a lifeline back to home base. I have to admit I hated being in the jungle. I found it claustrophobic and hated being constantly wet either through perspiration or rain. I just gritted my teeth and took it all on the chin. I found the best way to survive was with a little bit of banter and humour. Moving through it was worse when there was little tree cover and the sun shone through brightly. This led to the vegetation on the ground, flourishing and being extremely dense. We undertook fighting patrols and undertaking live firing exercises. It was hard work and I lost two stone by the end of the jungle phase.

The final Selection Phase was the Escape & Evasion & Tactical Questioning (TQ). The small number of us left around 10% of the original intake who had made it through endurance and jungle training now entered the final phase of selection. This phase was because of the likelihood of a special operation going wrong behind enemy lines is quite high, given the risks involved. The SAS requires soldiers who have the mental ability and spirit required to escape and evade capture and resist interrogation.

For the actual E&E (Escape and Evasion) portion of the course, we were given brief instructions on appropriate techniques. This even included talks from former POWs or Special Forces soldiers who have been in E&E situations in the real world. Before we were allowed to go out we were given a full search including a cavity search by medics, to ensure we had nothing stashed about our person. One trick a couple of the lads used was to swallow a tightly folded £20 note placed inside a condom. The idea was it would reappear in 24 hours, in one lad's case it appeared 36 hours later after the exercise had finished. We were then let loose in the countryside, wearing ill-fitting World War 2 vintage coats, boots and a small survival tin with instructions to make our way to a series of waypoints without being captured by the aptly named 'hunter force' made up of other soldiers. This portion lasted for three days after which, captured or not, we had to report for TQ (Tactical Questioning). Somehow, I managed to evade for the full three days, I to this day think it was sheer luck that I did not get found. I have never been so wet, cold and hungry as I was over those three days. One night I was so cold my teeth chatted and I shivered through the whole night.

The final part captured or not was TQ tests to test our ability to resist interrogation. I was treated roughly by the interrogators and often made to stand in 'stress positions' naked with a bag over my head for hours at a time, while disorientating white noise was blasted at me. After which it was my turn for questioning, I was to only answer with the so-called 'big 4' (name, rank, serial number and date of birth). All other questions must be answered with "I'm sorry, but I cannot answer that question." Failure to do so would result in me failing the course. The questions used all sorts of tricks to try and get a reaction from me. They acted friendly and then tried to get me to chat with them; or they would stand inches away from me and scream unfavourable remarks about the sexual habits of my mum. One female interrogator laughed at the size of my penis, trying to humiliate me as I stood in front of her naked. I realised a real interrogation would be a lot harsher and may well not get to leave alive when it was is all over. That said, days of interrogations and enduring the stress positions and white noise did break my own sense of time and reality.

With the selection phase over the four of us left, got our coveted beige beret with the distinctive winged dagger insignia. As a newly badged member of the Special Air Service, we all felt justly proud. We were still on probation and had much to prove and would be watched closely by the

DS during continuation training with one of the four of us being RTU'd during continuation training.

I was posted initially into B Squadron the same squadron made famous for storming the Iranian embassy in May 1980. I stayed with B Squadron most of my time whilst I was in the SAS. I made some good lifelong friends, some of whom I have lost, not just in action either. There are those that could not cope on civvy street or delayed PTSD (Post Traumatic Stress Disorder) caught up with them. PTSD is an anxiety disorder caused by very stressful, frightening or distressing events. The horrific images burnt into memory can haunt you for years and play tricks on your mind. It is a well-known fact that more soldiers committed suicide after returning from the Falklands than died in action. The effects of the two Iraq wars and Afghanistan have to fully filter through. It can be years before PTSD can catch up with you, and giving yourself a mental health check every now and again is not a bad thing. PTSD is a strange thing, it can creep up on you years later and have the strangest effects. Nightmares are a common one, but fear of going outside or still thinking you are in a war zone. For a few it all becomes too much and take their own lives.

As I settled into the SAS I realised how different being in the SAS was compared to the rest of the Army. You would see faces disappear for weeks or months, to reappear looking quite suntanned, without a word of where they had been or what they had done. You could wake up one morning and by the afternoon be travelling on a mission anywhere in the world. Being at Hereford is very much about being in a clandestine world and everything is pretty much on a 'need to know' basis. It is a constant hive of activity and the place has a real buzz about it

We spent hours in the killing house firing thousands of rounds has we practiced building clearance and hostage rescue. What was most amazing about the killing house was the walls with special rubber linings that caught every bullet and sent it into a tray at the bottom. Along with the killing house there was extensive weapons training on virtually every weapon in existence, including our very own C8 which I grew to admire.

The C8 was born out of the C7 when in 1984; Canada adopted a new 5.56 mm assault rifle. To avoid research and design expenses, the Canadians simply purchased the license from the USA for a new assault rifle, chambered for the latest 5.56 x 45 NATO ammunition. This was the Colt model 715, also known as the M16A1E1 rifle. Adopted as the C7, this rifle combined features from both earlier M16A1 rifles, such as full automatic fire mode and a two-position flip-up diopter sight, and from the newest M16A2, such as heavy barrel, rifled with faster 1:7 twist, better suited for 5.56mm NATO ammunition. Later on, Diemaco (now Colt Canada) developed a short-barrelled carbine version, fitted with telescoped buttstock, which was designated the C8. The very same weapon now used by the SAS to replace the M16 that was the standard SAS rifle. I personally think it is a better weapon than the standard UK forces SA80. It has much less working parts to contend with and clean. Operationally needs less gun oil and is less prone to stoppages. However, the SA80 is slightly more accurate over longer ranges. Although I am sure, a few of my fellow SAS colleagues would disagree. In the SAS you get your hands on a vast array of hardware from the Heckler & Koch 417, MP7 to an assortment of sidearms and shotguns. The SAS has an almost carte Blanche ability to buy any weapon that they need. They are also the first to try out any new weapon or weapon system before a much larger order is placed.

Other aspects of the training were more specialised such as VIP protection, advanced driving and covert intelligence gathering operations.

After a few national and international operations, it was time for our squadron to deploy to Afghanistan; some of us could end up doing seven tours in Afghanistan. I had already done one tour with the Para's so was not a total 'noob' when it came to the 'Stan'.

Chapter Three – Hit and Run

Afghanistan is a vast country and the role of the armed forces has been on an unprecedented scale due to the vast size and number of Taliban fighting to regain power and control of Afghanistan. Which they once ran under a regime of tyranny and fear. That those of us in the western world have not seen since the Second World War. Money and the opium trade are the biggest strangle hold the Taliban still has. Farmers get paid substantial amounts by the Taliban to grow poppies instead of food crops, this is the one area the Northern Alliance has struggled to combat and have any great impact on. When the majority of armed forces leaves Afghanistan in 2014, the country will either move forward or fall back into anarchy. I just hope the people of Afghanistan stay strong and can have the democratic society free of fear that they truly deserve after years of fighting. They have lost loved ones or even entire families to the war with Russia and then the war against the Taliban. Often being in the wrong place at the wrong time, getting caught up in the crossfire.

A Chinook had been dispatched from Camp Bastion - these 99ft long helicopters are still capable of 140-150 mph. Although, still a large enough and slow enough target for the Taliban to fire a few RPGs off. This means, they always require top cover from an Apache. The threat of RPGs and the odd ZSU-23 AA battery dotted about, meant threats to the aircraft were taken seriously. A well placed RPG could knock a Chinook out of the sky and heavily damage even the much more armoured Apache. So far during the war in Afghanistan, there have been 151 aircraft losses, 119 rotary wing and 32 fixed wing. Of these only 36 have been due to hostile fire though.

One story of an IRT mission has an Apache's camera recording an RPG passing 10 feet under a Chinook, and one passing 10 feet above the

Chinook as it came into land at the LZ (Landing Zone). The approaches to Bastion tended to be where the Taliban would try to get random pot shots off no matter what approach an aircraft chose to come in on.

The casualty we had on the ground had lost his arm, as an RPG had gone through the driver's side of the WMIK (Weapons Mount Installation Kit) taking the drivers arm off before exiting and exploding. All three had been lucky it had not exploded in the vehicle. Seconds after the RPG had exploded, we were in an intense firefight with the Taliban, whilst trying to get the wounded trooper out of the WMIK and give him immediate first aid.

The WMIK was used as reconnaissance and close fire support vehicles. The WMIK manufactured jointly by Land Rover and Ricardo Vehicle Engineering, featured a strengthened chassis and are stripped down before being fitted with roll cages and weapon mounts. Typically the vehicles can carry one 12.7 mm Heavy Machine Gun, 7.62 mm General Purpose Machine Gun (GPMG) or, on occasion the MILAN ATGM, on the rear ring-mount, with an additional pintle mounted GPMG on the front passenger side. In 2007, they were fitted with a new belt-fed Automatic Lightweight Grenade Launchers (ALGL) made by Heckler and Koch. Which could fire up to 360 grenades per minute with an effective range of 1.5 km and a maximum range of up to 2.2 km. The ALGL has proven to be a tasty and effective bit of kit.

This was a typical Taliban ambush – what they did not know, was that we had gone in to poke a stick and see what would happen. As the rifle and light machine gun fire became effective - we were all too aware it would not be long before mortar fire would start raining down on us. The signaller got on the net to request fire support and a medical evacuation. A Chinook and two Apaches were immediately dispatched to our location not far from Chora. Our medic needed to get trooper Harris stabilised and ready to go onto the back of the Chinook as soon as it landed.

The Chinook could only have 30-60 seconds on the deck before it would most likely be mortared or RPGs fired at it. The Chinooks were a real lifesaver and the crew on them, including the medical team were heroes. In the back of the Chinook, the medical team would actually start to operate on the route back to Bastion. Enduring the vibration and sudden movements the Chinook made – in order to avoid incoming fire. They are so focused the casualty they fail to notice the tracer rounds flashing past the Chinook's windows.

With the Chinook on its way, the two Apaches started to clear the LZ prior to the Chinook landing. As soon as the Chinook was away, they would then give us fire support. Within 15 minutes the Chinook was in the zone, the two rear door gunners opened up and took out two RPGs before they had a chance to fire – impressive stuff. Along with the Chinook, I could hear the distinctive sound of an Apache before it let off a full salvo of rockets at the main Taliban position. These two actions halved the fire that raining down on us.

In seconds the Chinook was on the deck, trooper Harris was hurriedly loaded into the back - before it quickly took off and sped off into the night. The Apaches stayed on station and cleared further pockets of resistance, whilst we made could use of their distraction and got out of the area - back into an area controlled by allied forces. Harris was saved and lived to fight another day, although with the loss of an arm his SAS days were over.

These hit and run type patrols were very reminiscent of the ones carried out by the original SAS under David Stirling in North Africa. Stirling thought and agreed that approaching by land under the cover of night would be safer and more effective than parachuting - after their disastrous first mission parachuting into the Libyan Desert. As quickly as possible Stirling organised raids on airfields and ports using this simple method, sometimes bluffing his way through checkpoints at night using the language skills of some of his soldiers.

Under his leadership, the Lewes bomb was invented by Jock Lewes - the first handheld dual explosive and incendiary device. American jeeps, which were able to deal with the harsh desert terrain better than other transport, were cut down, adapted and fitted with obsolete RAF Vickers machine guns. Stirling also pioneered the use of small groups to escape detection. Stirling often led from the front, his SAS units driving through enemy airfields to shoot up aircraft and crew, replacing the early operational strategy of planting Lewes bombs to enemy aircraft on foot.

In North Africa, during the fifteen months before Stirling's capture, the SAS had destroyed over 250 aircraft on the ground, dozens of supply dumps, wrecked railways and telecommunications, and had put hundreds of enemy vehicles out of action. Montgomery of Alamein described Stirling as 'mad, quite mad' but admitted that men like Stirling were needed in time of war.

The SAS pioneered the use of the Land Rover as a mobile weapons platform. In Iraq, the SAS used Land Rovers to move across the desert in order to find Scud missile launchers and destroy them. The biggest problem with the WMIK in Afghanistan was its poor survivability – especially when it came to IEDs. They offered about as much protection as a piece of tin foil. Much has been written in the press about the issues of the poor protection that they offered. Three members of 23 SAS and Corporal Sarah Bryant, 26 were killed when their Snatch Land Rover was blown up by an improvised explosive device in June 2008 near to Lashkar

Gah. Cpl Bryant became the first female British soldier to be killed in Afghanistan.

The Land Rover was conceived by the Rover Company in 1947 during the aftermath of World War II and is as iconic as the SAS in many ways. It was Maurice Wilks Rover's chief designer who came up with the plan to produce a light agricultural and utility vehicle. It was of a similar concept to the highly successful American Willys Jeep used in the war, but with an emphasis on agricultural use. The Land Rover entered production in 1948 with what was later termed the Series I. In May 1949 the Ministry of War placed a first order of 1878 vehicles from then on it has progressed through the Series II, Forward Control IIa/IIb, Series III, Defender and finally the SNATCH and Wolf based on the Defender 110.

However, with us using them mainly as an off road vehicle meant the IEDs are less of a threat, as most IEDs are placed on the main roads, supply roads, track or bridges. They can be set in positions to target either troops or vehicles. We still needed to be vigilant though off-road and carry out various operational checks. Off road, we had to be more concerned about running into an old Russian minefield that is not on our map. The other concern was with the WMIK and its narrow wheels, which can cause it to struggle to transverse some of the off-road ground found in Afghanistan. The WMIKs speed and being relatively lightweight is an advantage in a Special Forces role.

We made it out of the area unscathed and not one bullet hole in any vehicle or any other casualty. Another night, another successful operation and we had taken the war directly to a Taliban occupied area and harassed them a little.

Chapter Four – Big city fight

We left Kandahar airport from our accommodation aptly called "Blade House". 'Blade' being the term coming from the SAS designation as Sabre squadrons of its four fighting subunits A, B, D and G. In our WMIKs, we joined the early evening rush hour. Before we weaved our WMIKs through the traffic, in the hustle and bustle of a normal busy weekday in Kandahar.

Kandahar or Qandahar (Pashto/Persian, known in older literature as Candahar, is the second largest city in Afghanistan, with a population of about 512,200. Kandahar is the capital of the Kandahar Province, located in the south of the country at about 3,297 ft above sea level. The Arghandab River runs along the west of the city.

Kandahar is one of the most culturally significant cities of the Pashtuns and has been their traditional seat of power for more than 200 years. It is a major trading centre for sheep, wool, cotton, silk, felt, food grains, fresh and dried fruit, and tobacco. The region produces fine fruits, especially pomegranates and grapes, and the city has plants for canning, drying, and packing fruit. Kandahar has extensive road links with Lashkar Gah and Herat to the west, Ghazni and Kabul to the northeast, Tarinkot to the north, and Quetta in neighbouring Balochistan to the south.

The region around Kandahar is one of the oldest known human settlements. Alexander the Great had laid-out the foundation of what is now Old Kandahar in the 4th century BC, and gave it the Ancient Greek name Alexandria of Arachosia. Many empires have long fought over the city due to its strategic location along the trade routes of southern, central and western Asia. In 1709, Mirwais Hotak made the region an independent kingdom and turned Kandahar into the capital of the Hotaki dynasty. In 1747, Ahmad Shah Durrani, founder of the last Afghan empire, made it the capital of modern Afghanistan.

Our convoy did its best to cut through the heavy traffic, as we made our way to the objective on the fringe of the city. Our mission was to launch a raid on yet another compound in the North. As we made our way, the usual steady banter kept everyone's nerves in check. Although we still needed to be alert as attacks on convoys were still quite common, some sections of the city being worse than others.

We met up with our Delta Force counterparts at a laying up point just over a mile from the objective. Delta had arrived in their Humvee's complete with FRAG 5 armour kit. The FRAG 5 armour kit upgrade includes a much heavier 600-pound door and additional armour plating at key points on the vehicle. Although the use of Humvee's, has recently become more restricted due to low resistance to IED attacks.

Today's operations were to be a joint operation and our target had been homed in on and tracked via the satellite phone that he used. The street faced onto some dusty open ground before some dense vegetation and more houses. It was across this dusty open ground we would begin our assault. It was a dangerous operation and resistance could well be fierce. The whole area was thought to be significantly dangerous enough for a couple of warrior tanks to be on hand to support our attack if needed.

It was now dark and not all of us had night vision goggles due to the small number that we had available at the time. The Warriors had night vision capability, as did the Delta force soldiers who were in an 'overwatch' position to make use of more powerful night-vision equipment and give long range fire support.

We had two compounds to hit with each being attacked simultaneously by two separate patrols. The compounds were labelled Blade 1 and Blade 2. I was allocated to Blade 2 - Captain Wesson, our boss who had only been with the troop for a few months, was leading the Blade 2 assault.

Wesson had been in the Army six years, he was the stereotypical public schoolboy, but this had not made him arrogant in any way. To the contrary, he was very down to earth and could swear like the best of us. So far had proven to be a half-decent 'Rupert' and gained our respect. He was aggressive and resourceful in battle - he would not send his men anywhere he would not go himself.

We went prone and waited for the order to commence the assault. Assaulting buildings is something we practice time after time back at the 'Killing House' in Hereford. We practiced it to the point of total boredom, but that meant, we were all very slick when the time came to do it for real. Instinct is much quicker than having to think - even a few milliseconds can be the difference between life and death.

We ran across the sand with our boots struggling to get a proper grip as they sank into the soft dusty soil, before arriving at the front of the compound and prepared to go in.

As we burst into the compound - we were hit with a hail of bullets, followed by an RPG being fired directly at us. Within minutes, half of us had been hit taking bullets in our legs, arms and bottom. I did my best to carry out battlefield first aid on one of the casualties.

Several other SAS troopers moved up onto a building roof across the street from the compound so they could give direct fire support. The amount of fire being poured on us meant the assault ground to a halt and we needed to retreat. We managed to ex-filtrate without any more injuries, before realising that Sergeant Jones was still just inside laying in the courtyard with blood pumping out of a bullet wound in his thigh. With a man down and inside, there was no way the Warriors and the Delta force guys could obliterate the compound. It was now a case of who would finish off Jones first - his wounds or the Taliban? Without a thought for my own safety I ran back in with another trooper to drag Jones out. Our boss shouted at us to stop, fearing it was far too dangerous to go back inside and did not want any more casualties. We ignored his plea and did our best to dodge the bullets from an AK-47 being fired from inside the compound and dragged Jones out by his blood covered arms.

The Kalashnikov assault rifle more commonly known as the AK-47 or just AK (Avtomat Kalashnikova – 47, translates to the Kalashnikov automatic rifle, model 1947), and its derivatives. It had been and still is with minor modifications, manufactured in dozens of countries, and has been used in hundreds of countries and conflicts since its introduction. The total number of the AK-type rifles made worldwide during the last 60 years is estimated at 90+ million. The AK47 is known for its simplicity of operation, ruggedness and maintenance, and unsurpassed reliability even in the most inhospitable of conditions.

The AK story began late in 1942, when Soviet troops captured several of the then new German MKb.42 machine carbine, along with some 7.92 ammunition. By mid-1943 Soviet experts had evaluated the MKb.42 along with US-supplied M1carbine and it was decided at a high level that similar weapons, firing similar ammunition, must be developed for the Soviet army as soon as possible.

After the war in 1946, the AK-46 was presented for official military trials. In 1947, the fixed-stock version was introduced into service with the odd Soviet Army unit. One early development of the design was the AKS (S meaning Skladnoy or "folding"), which was equipped with an underfolding metal shoulder stock. The AK-47 was officially accepted by the Soviet Armed Forces in 1949 and used by the majority of the member states of the Warsaw Pact.

Throughout the World - the AK and its variants are among the most commonly smuggled small arms sold to governments, rebels, criminals, and civilians alike. In some countries, prices for AKs are very low; in Somalia, Rwanda, Mozambique, Congo and Tanzania prices are between $30 and $125 per weapon, and prices have fallen in the last few decades due to mass counterfeiting.

With Jones and everyone now clear of the compound, it was left to Major McCapin to consider our options. There was still fire coming from Blade 2 and now another building had opened up. He discussed various options with the Americans. It was decided that we would assault the new building that had opened up, whilst Delta Force cleared our original objective. The warriors opened up with a 30mm RARDEN cannon and pummelled the target. Before Delta Force went in to finish off any remaining resistance. A couple of M1 Abrahams tanks had been put on standby just in case.

Our assault on the building further down the street went as planned and we cleared it room by room. We met only light resistance and captured two and killed one Taliban insurgent.

Delta Force had now finally cleared Blade 2, which was pretty much a pile of rubble and bodies. The first flicker of light as dawn approached revealed a scene of complete chaos and carnage. In daylight, this would become an even more dangerous place as the locals awoke to find us there would pass it on to the Taliban. We knew we needed to get out of the area quickly. Thankfully, Sergeant Jones survived, his blood loss had been great and even with plasma being pumped into him in the back of the Chinook it had been touch and go. The bullet had exited very close the femoral artery, if the bullet had it that I am sure it would have been 'game over' for him. .

Delta Force took all the prisoners off our hands and we mounted our WMIK's for the trip back to the 'Blade House'. We learnt some hard lessons from the attack and that the Taliban in the area were better equipped and offered more resistance than we thought. Experience and expertise is still no match for raw firepower and a number advantage. The Taliban had both the raw firepower and number advantage during the initial assault. Fire support is great providing you can get it down without injuring or killing your own soldiers if they are in the blast radius.

The term danger close is in relation close air support, artillery, mortar, and naval gunfire support fires, it is the term included in the method of engagement segment of a call for fire, which indicates that friendly forces are within close proximity of the target. The close proximity distance is determined by the weapon and munitions fired.

For instance, the 60mm mortar has a blast radius of about 20 - 25 meters. The 81/82 MM has a blast radius of 35 - 40 meters and the 120mm/122mm mortar has a blast radius of about 60 meters. An operation like this shows how well the allied forces work together, notwithstanding the banter and competitive nature of the armed forces especially Special Forces.

Chapter Five - Takedown

Another night and another typical takedown - we had got ourselves up at 3.30pm to get ourselves prepared for the night's operation. The plan and the target changed at least three times before we were due to go. Much to the annoyance of us and the supporting aircrew tasked with getting us in and out. We set off in the early evening darkness in a Chinook with two Apaches providing top cover. It was about 100Km journey to the target area some 50km from Laskar Gah in Helmand province. It would be a hot location and we would all need to be on our toes and out the back of the Chinook. As we got in close and I looked out of the window, I could see tracer fire coming up from the Taliban fighters below. Our target tonight was another intelligence officer, which was part of a much larger Mi6 effort targeting terrorism. There are strong links between Al-Qaeda and the Taliban. Fighters from across the world have joined the Taliban as part of their Jihad (religious duty) to help drive the allied forces out of Afghanistan. The SAS, along with the rest of the SF (Special Forces) in Afghanistan are prime targets for the Taliban to kill; their hatred of us was much higher than the average soldier and a source of propaganda to kill one of us.

The mission was all about trying to find out further information regarding the pipeline of foreign fighters into Afghanistan. Many came across the Pakistan border to the front line in Afghanistan. D Squadron who had been in Afghanistan prior to us and found some of these raids very difficult, on many occasions as they approached the target locals had spotted them, using anything they could find to make a noise to alert the Taliban of their presence. This led to a hard assault, with the Taliban now alerted and firing assault rifles at D Squadron from only a few feet, in what became very short-range firefight.

Quick thinking was essential - you had to think and fire pretty much at the same time or be shot. Since these raids, we have tried to blend in often by disguising ourselves as locals. By blending in and choosing the correct time and day to perform, an assault helped us become much more covert. On a couple of occasions we did not even get to fire a shot - getting in making a hard arrest, before getting out without anyone knowing.

Tonight was similar fair, although the American Marines and a SEAL team were on hand to support us. Resistance was expected to be high on this assault. The Taliban here had a mixture of light and heavy weapons along with RPGs. This particular target had been tracked by MI6 for some months know including various moves around the globe to Pakistan and other Arab countries.

In total, there were to be eight SAS operatives involved in this assault along with a SEAL team and American fire support in the form of a few Bradley tanks and an AC130 Spooky on station to both observe and offer fire support if required. Some of the lads hated working with the American's, but I enjoyed it. There was a mutual respect between the SF forces, if a little rivalry when it came down to individual missions. The American planners do hold the SAS in high esteem though. They know we are a highly skilled and capable force. Odd ones over the years have held preference of the SAS even over Delta Force.

The assault tonight was made slightly more complex due to a minefield in some open ground just to the left of the compound. This meant that the assault options were narrowed and would need to almost zigzag up to the objective.

The Chinook came down steeply before settling on the deck before we all ran down the ramp into the helicopters downwash. The first priority was to find some cover before the Chinook took off again and silence descended on our LZ. Via the net the SEAL team was already in their FUP (Forming Up Point) and the C130 Spooky on station gathering intelligence and acting as an 'overwatch' for all the ground forces.

We made our way to our own FUP, from where we would launch the attack. The SEAL team was acting as spotters and would also capture anyone trying to flee the compound. As we got to about 200 metres from the objective, we held firm for a short period of time - to get eyes on the target and formulate a final plan. We would then break up into two patrols of four and move on the compound from two different angles.

The patrol I was with, would go from the right and the other team circled round to the left, circumventing the minefield before moving onto the compound. It was a dark starless night, which helped with us being covert, at the same time, made it harder for us to see even with the help of night vision goggles. Night vision goggles are great, but they do rob some of your peripheral vision.

As we moved in an explosion and hysterical screams suddenly interrupted the silence. One SAS trooper in another patrol had walked into a small group of trees and stepped on a land mine. It had blown his lower limbs clean off and alerted the Taliban to our presence.

We now had a man down - lying critically injured in a potential minefield not on our map and the Taliban had begun to lay down quite effective fire. The SEAL team sprang into action and made their way to where the injured SAS operative was. We started to return fire at the Taliban firing from the roof, the AC130 then opened up its GAU-12/U Equalizer which is a is a five-barrel 25 mm Gatling-type rotary cannon. These cannons can also be found mounted on fighter jets, such as the AV-8B Harrier II and other land-based fighting vehicles.

It made light work of the Taliban on the roof and suppressed the fire enough for us to get closer. Regardless of having, a man down we had a mission and an objective to complete. Stevo could still be heard groaning, but to get to him out the area would need to be searched for any more mines, before any rescue could be undertaken.

Now only a few metres from the compound, the Spooky above was still giving bursts of the GAU-12, causing small dust clouds as the bullets hit the compound roof and walls. We ordered it to stand down to ensure there was no blue on blue. Which meant it would now be down to us, to do a room-by-room clearance.

Initially there was no resistance and no one to be found - we cleared each room and found nothing, it was as if they had all vanished or all been killed on the compound roof. The compound roof was littered with several blood stained bodies. The target must have fled prior to our arrival and all that had been left was a small group of dead fighters with no real intelligence value. Any intelligence they may of had had been taken with them to the grave.

We found a few IEDs and some RPGs, but nothing of any great intelligence use. With the compound secure, a rescue could start for Stevo - getting him out of the minefield before he bled to death. The strange part about blown off limbs is that they do not always bleed as expected, and they tended to just ooze blood more often than not. The oozing is enough if not given medical attention to lead to shock and possibly death. Shock is the biggest killer after any major trauma; this is why the 'golden hour' is so important. The Golden hour is a reference to the time period lasting from a few minutes to several hours following traumatic injury being sustained by a casualty, during which there is the highest likelihood that prompt medical treatment will prevent death. The sooner we can get them back to a medical facility like the one at Camp Bastion the chances of survival are increased greatly.

To check for mines it was a case of doing a barma and then getting down on your belt buckle and softly removing soil from where the Vallon had given an indication. It was a slow process and with each section cleared. Mine tape was placed either side of the track to indicate a safe area to walk. It took nearly an hour to get to Stevo, who by now was semi-conscious. The next issue was getting Stevo out and back down the narrow track between the mine tape.

Barma or Operation Barm is the Army name given to the procedure of searching the ground of IEDs using visual checks and the Vallon metal detector. It is carried out on foot by the lead person who walks in front of the troop or vehicles.

Stevo was a well built and heavy lad, dragging him out was not really an option, he needed to be carried out on a makeshift stretcher that the SEAL team had cobbled together. The SEAL team even offered to go and get him, whilst we got ready to move out to a new extraction point that would take us and Stevo out. The new extraction point was too small for a Chinook so an American Black Hawk was called in to transport us out. It took three of the SEAL team nearly 20 minutes to stabilise and get Steveo away from the minefield. With Steveo out myself and four others took up stretcher duty and made out way to the extraction point.

Minus both his legs, Steveo made a full recovery in hospital. He was one of those guys that could bounce back from anything. Even losing his limbs did not stop him running, and even entering a couple of marathons 18 months after he was injured. An example to us all of a true hero.

Chapter Six – Factory fitted

In the back of a dark C130, with only the soft moonlight giving any form of light my eyes still adjusting to the dark, I shuffled towards the ramp along with the rest of the assault force and prepared to jump. I could feel the cold air seeping through my combats now that the ramp was fully lowered. With a parachute on my back, my C8 strapped to my side and all my assault equipment to my front. It was hard to keep my balance as the C130 pitched up and down slightly.

I stepped off the ramp and into the night's sky and after a short fall deployed my parachute for a HAHO (High Altitude High Opening) jump. This type of jump meant we would use our chutes to glide for quite a few km away from the noise of the Hercules, and get closer to our intended target unnoticed. Strapped to the front of one of the lads was a German Shepard. Dogs are known as man's best friend and in a war zone have proved invaluable in keeping soldiers safe, lately in both Iraq and Afghanistan. Spaniels have been used as bomb disposal dogs able to sniff out explosives. German Shepards have been used not only as guard dogs, but also track and capture insurgents. It's estimated that the Germans used a total of nearly thirty thousand dogs during World War I. They had six thousand on the front lines and four thousand, in reserve at the beginning of the war.

The SAS has been parachuting them more recently into enemy strongholds in Afghanistan with Taliban-seeking German shepherds strapped to their chests. German Shepherds are a relatively new breed of dog, with their origin dating to 1899. As part of the Herding Group, German Shepherds are working dogs developed originally for herding sheep. Since that time, however, because of their strength, intelligence, trainability and obedience, German Shepherds around the world are often the preferred breed for many types of work, including search-and-rescue, police and military roles. The breed was actually created by the crossbreeding of working sheep dogs from rural Germany by an ex cavalry officer called Max von Stephanitz whose aim was to create a working dog for herding which could trot for long periods.

Once on the ground, the dogs are let off as forward scouts to go and search buildings for any Taliban fighters. To aid in keeping track of the dog and to gather intelligence before the SAS move in, the dogs have cameras strapped to their head's. These cameras stream live video back that the SAS operator can view and even replay the feed to aid in an assault or in search of IEDs. It is dangerous work, and several dogs have been killed in action. By giving their lives, they have saved the lives of soldier's. The training of these dogs is not too dissimilar to the way police dogs are trained. The big difference with the Special Forces dogs are that they are trained for High Altitude High Opening jumps. The SAS dogs are trained to jump tethered to their handlers from heights as high as 25,000 feet and up to 20 miles away – undertaking a 30 minute glide to their objective. The high altitude and risk of hypoxia, means the dogs have to wear special oxygen masks. It was Delta Force who originally trained dogs to make HAHO jumps.

Our target tonight was a major IED making facility a few miles from Jalalabad and towards the Pakistani border. It was reported that one of the Taliban's top bomb makers were also due to be there. We silently came in and landed just short of the bomb factory, packed our chutes up and made our way to the factory, hitting it shortly after 3am. It was a textbook raid, with the three four man patrols entering simultaneously, in a not too dissimilar fashion to the raid on the Libyan embassy in London, with maybe a little less pizazz. The team I was with entered via the rear of the building, a variation of the normal compound, although this compound had smaller compounds within it, such was the size of the compound. A large wall surrounded it, with two large metal entrance gates.

Rather than take the gates out and alert our presence before we needed to – we simply climbed the walls and each team made its way to one of the three inner compounds. Once inside our compound it was off eerily quiet. We moved in expecting fire at any minute and it was not long before all hell broke loose. Rifle fire seemed to be opening up from all angles. Rounds were bouncing off the wall behind us with bits of flying stone hitting the back of my neck. The wall behind me quickly became badly pockmarked. The German Shepard with the other team called Jake, had already scouted ahead and found a few of the positions before the Taliban had opened up on him. Amazingly Jake had made it back out alive and is handler was loathe to send him back in. Jake was barking his head off still and could just be heard over the din of gunfire, almost as if he was angry that he could not get back in amongst the action.

Corporal Warwick to my right got the first kill with a perfectly aimed shot - straight through the head. With one down and several more to go, we continued to fire back and move forward. I got the next confirmed shot with a bullet through the shoulder and a second in the chest – another AK47 silenced. We moved up the stairs with still quite a large amount of fire and Captain Wesson decided to pop off a grenade and took three Taliban out in one explosion - as the blast and shrapnel ripped them apart. The force of the blast had ripped the arm and all the clothes off one of the Taliban fighters. Another had his guts hanging out.

One by one, the Taliban fell without a single round touching any one of us much to our amazement. We continued to push forward and had the house cleared in what seemed like minutes, but turned out to be nearly half an hour. With the building cleared, we went firm, whilst waiting for updates from the other two patrols clearing the other two compounds. We did not have to wait long for the other two teams to give the all clear. With the compound clear, we began our search for intelligence – this included searching and photographing each body for intelligence purposes. We spent a further 30 minutes gathering intelligence before it was time to make good our escape.

Some of us did wonder if it would not have been better just to have brought an F16 in with a bomb and flattened the place in one go, but the compound was far too close to civilian and the risk of injuring or even killing a local was far too high. However, it was a successful mission, which would save the lives of a few more allied soldiers. We seized much of the smaller bomb components and explosives for intelligence use. This latest batch of IEDs being produced had the usual saw blade conductors replaced with strips of graphite. These low metal content IEDs as they were known, were virtually impossible to find with the Vallon the standard British way to detect IEDs.

The Vallon works using two different detection methods for the detection of unexploded ordnance or metal-cased mines.

The first is the active pulse induction method. This helps with the detection of unexploded ordnance detection in mineralized soils where magnetometers would give too many false alarms. Likewise, for a quick search of sub munitions and shells, the Vallons large search head, combined with a special unexploded ordnance signal processing in the metal detector, improves efficiency.

The search head on the Vallon continuously emits electromagnetic pulses. Between each magnetic pulse is a short pause. During these pauses the electromagnetic reaction from metal objects, influenced by the search head, is detected by the detector.

The reaction time depends on the size of the metallic objects and the distance to the search head. The receiver in the detectors processes this response and converts it to an alarm signal.

The second method used is the gradient magnetometer Method. The magnetic field of the earth is homogeneous with regards to the field strength and the direction of the field strength. If a ferromagnetic object is brought into this homogeneous field, the 'own field' of the object is superposing the local magnetic field of the earth, hence creating a distortion.

As the distance from the object increases, the field distortion is decreased. The extent of the distortion depends on several factors. The most important ones are the size of the object to be detected and its permeability. If the buried object is magnetized, i.e. It has an own magnetic field, the field lines are reacting according to the polarity of the object. In general, the total disturbance of magnetized objects is larger than the disturbance of objects having no field. On rare occasions, the total disturbance might even be smaller, depending on the object orientation towards the terrestrial magnetic field.

Unexploded ordnance detectors are differential magnetometers, i.e. two sensors are arranged in geometrically true alignment at a set distance. They are connected in a way that they will measure the value zero in a homogeneous field. Each sensor passing a ferrous object is differently affected.

As can be seen the Vallon relies on metal based ordnance in order to detect it. The Americans have ground radar based systems that can detect any type of IED even low metal content ones.

We had a 3km trek back to where our usual taxi, in the form of a Chinook would take us back to Kandahar. The 3km trek was undertaken in total silence including radio silence, as the last thing we wanted was to alert the Taliban to our presence and end up in a full on fighting retreat back to the extraction point.

The fast paced walk back to the extraction point helped keep us warm - being February it was not uncommon for temperatures to be in the minus figures especially at night. The Afghanistan climate can be very harsh with extreme heat and extreme cold depending on the time of year. The coldest month on average is January and the hottest July and August.

Afghanistan receives an average of 316 mm of rain per year this compares with the UK's average of 854mm and the North American average of 767 mm.

Chapter Seven – Aviation Disaster

We had a midnight brief before we climbed aboard a couple of Black Hawks ready for the mission. Nearly twenty minutes later we were coming down onto our objective as we made the final approach to the LZ. The LZ that had been identified by the lead Black Hawks pilot. The second Black Hawk, was just over a disc behind the first as this point. The Black Hawk dropped down to 300 feet after passing some power lines and we began to land. It was at this point the helicopter crew realised we were off target and about to land in the wrong field.

They had to make a snap decision - they could have flown forward, circled around and come in again. The lead Black Hawk decided instead to fly backwards, in doing so, it kicked up a large cloud of dust hiding it from view. The second Black Hawk then carried out the same manoeuvre without being able to see properly the lead Black Hawk.

I was on the lead Black Hawk and we were soon on the ground, jumping out of the side door. Just after I had jumped out the tail rotor on the other Black Hawk touched and the rotor blade sliced off the tail boom on the Black Hawk I had just been in. The other Black Hawk was a few metres above the ground, and the contact with the other Black Hawk caused it to tip from side to side violently enough, for two of the SAS operatives to fall out of the now open side door and crashed to the ground. The Black Hawk then crashed to the ground before tipping over on its side. It had just missed the two men who had fallen out as it tipped over.

As the Black Hawk tipped over and the rotor blades dug into the ground and shattered sending debris out in all directions, which caused a few injuries. The lads that had fallen out of the Black Hawk were untouched, as was the pilot of the Black Hawk that had just crashed. A couple of the crew inside had suffered some minor cuts and bruises though. The rest of the injuries were easy enough to deal with, but the op was now off as we now had two helicopter crews to keep safe.

The badly damaged Black Hawks needed to be destroyed to ensure nothing fell into enemy hands. On the less badly damaged of the two we stuck some explosive in the fuel tank and the second on its side, placed some explosive underneath. The hope was that the explosion and subsequent fire from the aviation fuel would be enough to destroy both. The explosion that followed the detonation of the explosives caused quite a high and billowing plumes of orange flame followed by thick black smoke.

By now, the helicopter crew and the rest of the SAS troop were already a kilometre away. We realised that blowing up the Black Hawks would further alert the Taliban to our presence. We were now in an escape and evasion scenario, to get to a suitable LZ for a Chinook to get us all out.

This was not the first helicopter incident the SAS had suffered; we have lost men to helicopter crashes before. One nasty one in Iraq before my time was when a Puma helicopter flying out to drop some SAS operatives at an LZ. They were escorted by Lynx helicopters and it had been an uneventful flight out to the target. No direct or indirect fire or even signs of tracer fire from the ground below. As soon as they got to the target, insurgents became alerted to their presence and started firing. There fire was quite heavy or though ineffective. Through night vision goggles, the pilot could see insurgents could move into the cover of trees below.

The target of the mission was an insurgent leader and his 2IC (second in command). A local informant had spotted him going into the house that they were about to raid and tipped off the CIA. The Lynx helicopters flying with the Puma's were there to protect the Puma and also take out any escaping vehicles. Just like the Apache now does with Chinooks.

The door gunner opened the Puma's door and let rip with his gun; fire from the ground became more intense the radio crackled with reports as the pilot shouted that it was now hot and dynamic, meaning they were under fire and had to dodge the bullets.

The OC decided to get the men on the ground as quickly as possible. The Puma became engulfed in dust as it tried to land, so the pilot decided on a last minute change, but realising that a Lynx helicopter was passing right over them, the pilot decided to go up and then down quickly. In order to avoid the Lynx - the Puma came down a bit too quickly and slammed into the ground, rolling over onto its side. The force of the impact threw men out of the helicopter's side door. It was then realised that three men were actually trapped under the helicopter - two SAS operatives and a helicopter crew member.

Those that had escaped quickly regrouped to plan a rescue attempt. The two SAS operatives were rescued and quickly tendered to by the medics. Then the flames started to lick around the helicopter gearbox and a helicopter crew member was still trapped. Try as they might the other two that were trapped could not be shifted. In moments, flames engulfed the helicopter and soon rounds from the door-mounted machine gun were cooking off along with the whoosh of burning flares. It was too hot and too dangerous for anyone to get close. All anyone could do was stand and watch the horrific sight and smell - as the two trapped men were burnt alive.

With all of us now regrouped, Captain Wesson with some other NCO's put together a quick plan to evacuate us to a safe area for a rescue. We only had walking wounded and the greater the distance we could put between us and the destroyed Black Hawks the better. We had got an evacuation point, but it was 10km from our position, which meant a long walk before dawn.

The area was a mixture of fields with the odd treeline. Where possible we made use of dead ground or wadis to hide our movement. Keeping away from any tracks, as we had neither the time nor the equipment to search for any potential IEDs.

I will give the American helicopter crews credit, that they had no problems keeping up with our fast pace and were switched on. As planned, we arrived the Evac point just before dawn, and took cover whilst we waited for our ride home.

Chapter Eight – Firefight from Hell

As the sounds of gunfire echoed around the area, back at HQ they were formulating a new plan. These Taliban fighters had no intention of moving, they wanted to kill as many of us before they were killed themselves. Not too dissimilar to the Japanese in World War 2, who would fight to the bitter end - surrender was not an option.

Almost as soon as we had jumped off the ramp of the helicopter, we set up a perimeter around the helicopter as the rest of the troop got off. We then checked our maps as the Chinook lifted off. Within seconds, the first bullets were zipping passed our head. We quickly moved out as initially we were unable to spot the enemy position, being in a rockier and mountainous area near the Pakistan border. All we could do was get into better cover and return fire in the direction the bullets were coming from.

We found a small ridgeline a few metres high and got behind that. Our sergeant got up and was scanning the area when a mortar round exploded several meters in front of him causing him to duck. Finally, as we crawled to the top of the ridgeline we saw several black-clad Taliban fighters a few hundred metres ahead of us silhouetted against the night sky. We quickly got ourselves set up and the sergeant made sure the snipers and spotters were teamed up and ready to go, whilst the boss got on the net to give a sitrep, Army speak for situation report. A sniper got the first Taliban fighter and we saw him being pulled away by another Taliban fighter.

We made the decision to continue to stay put and take out as many of the enemy as we could see, then use the small amount of mortars we had with us to give some indirect fire on Taliban positions. We had an Apache about to lift off from Camp Bastion, but that was twenty minutes away. Twenty minutes in a firefight was a long time. As more Taliban seemed to start firing on us the first RPGs started to hit the ridgeline, showering shrapnel and rock fragments on us.

The fire was becoming more intense and more effective and it was becoming obvious we would be overwhelmed and overrun quite soon. The boss had to make a quick decision, which was to drop our bergan and get the hell out of there, ensuring nothing of any value to the Taliban was left in any bergan, I crammed anything of any use into the side pouches that unzipped of the bergan. These pouches attached to a yoke and became what is known as a rocket pack, due to that they looked like a rocket back on your back. The amount of resistance we were encountering was far higher than had been anticipated by our planners. The boss got on the net and told them what we were doing.

We moved off and got ourselves into a much better defensive position a few hundred meters that would suffice whilst we waited for air support. The plan was to use the slight drop in enemy fire due to the air support and get the hell out of there on our toes, as fast as we could.

By now, thousands of bullets had been fired at us and not one had found a target, the RPGs and mortar fire had got more effective and close to our position. If we had stayed on the ridgeline it was only a matter of time before a mortar scored a direct hit. As we got into our new position, there was only a small respite before the new wave of Taliban positions opened up from various crevices in the surrounding rocky area. We returned fire and finally got a few mortars off that scored some direct hits in quite quick succession. We were so focused on the fierce firefight and dodging RPGs and a hail of bullets, we did not notice the Apache that had appeared on station and was already letting rip with its 30mm chain gun, whilst taking some fire of its own. The crew could see that we had become surrounded and had nowhere to go, so it had come in quite close to draw some of the fire as well as fire back on the Taliban positions.

By now we had taken some casualties, nothing serious, just a few shrapnel wounds and cuts from bullets that had gotten a little too close. I won't mind saying that as the battle raged on, it was absolutely terrifying. It was the fiercest battle I had ever been in and never was eclipsed. The amount of fire that the Taliban had, was immense, it just kept on coming. The bullets were easy enough to dodge, but the RPGs and especially the mortars were something different.

Without the Apache, we would have been dead, without a doubt. Whilst the Apache could not clear all the fighters it dealt with the RPGs and mortar positions quite quickly, leaving us to deal with the small arms fire. My boss decided that four of us which included me, were to move out of our position and try to flank the enemy as best we could. Being surrounded meant taking out the positions behind us first.

We would need to move fast and hit the Taliban fighters before they were aware we were there. With covering fire from our position, we would circle back around and take out as many of the Taliban as we could. It sounded so simple, the key was to maintain momentum and not get bogged down. The minute we got bogged down, the Taliban would pump in more fighters into our location and the element of surprise would be lost.

We carefully claimed our way up and over the various rock to the higher positions the Taliban was in. It was slow progress to ensure we were not noticed and used any cover as best as we could. Just as we were about to get to the top, we saw on a ridgeline, a Taliban fighter huddle behind a rock and firing down on the rest of the troop. One shot from Barnes right into the side of his head and another position was silenced. We moved along the ridge swiftly, but silently, taking out each position we came across. They never saw us coming - such was their tunnel vision as they continued to give quick bursts of fire on the rest of our troop.

With eight under our belt some being killed in pairs as two of us shot them both simultaneously. This was where all the rounds fired and weapons training we had done, so we could be expert marksmen really came into its own.

By now, the Apache had left us, after getting low on fuel and ammunition, but we were gaining a foothold. An AC 130 Spooky was not that far out, after being sent to us from another operation. With the spooky on station the remaining Taliban fighters would not stand a chance. The upgraded AC-130U "Spooky" as well as the single 25 mm GAU-12 Equalizer also has a 40 mm L/60 Bofors cannon and a 105 mm M102 howitzer. These are all mounted on the left hand side of the aircraft.

We were still working our way along the ridgeline and killing Taliban fighters, until finally a position across from us finally saw us and changed their firing position. I took a bullet in the shoulder just above the ballistic plate in my chest armour. It was a hot stinging sensation as the bullet entered and then exited.

The force threw me off balance and I dropped one hand off my weapon, stumbling back slightly. The shriek I had made about being hit caused Barnes standing next to me, to shout "Fuck! Stone's been hit." Barnes quickly got me behind a rock and pulled my body armour off to check for holes. Other than a painful shoulder I did not feel too bad as Barnes slapped a bandage on the entry and the exit portion of the wound. Patched up and with the adrenaline still flowing, I found I had no difficulty carrying on the fight, although had to use my left shoulder for the butt of my weapon.

Barnes had been in the regiment for eight years and had pretty much seen it all, initially he had spent his time with the mobility troop before moving over to air troop. He joined the regiment with just over three years' service in the Welsh Guards and he was originally from Wales. He was a real racing snake lean and very mean, catch him in a bad mood and you were guaranteed to be punched. In battle, he was a cool and collected as you could be a real fighting man and natural warrior. He lived and breathed the Army, having no time for relationships. I have no idea what he will do, when the time comes for him to leave the regiment.

With disaster averted we went back to eliminating enemy positions just as the spooky laid down fire starting with a couple of shots from the 105mm cannon to take out two larger positions. Even from a few hundred metres away we could feel the ground shake and the subsequent blast wave, felt like a strong hot wind on our faces.

With a few more well placed rounds from the 25 mm Gatling gun and 40mm Bofors cannon. This silenced a few more positions before those that were left fled the scene, realising that we now had the advantage.

The Taliban must have known we were coming or we had stepped into a heavily defended area. All I knew was that I was starting to feel like shit and a little light headed. My mouth had gone totally dry and I felt slightly nauseous. The boss toyed with the idea of collecting our bergans, but decided that he could not put it past the Taliban to have booby trapped a few of them as they left the area.

In a matter of minutes, we were making our way to an LZ under the watchful eye of the spooky still flying above. Back at Camp Bastion, I was patched up and taken off operational duties for two weeks. I could have gone home, but felt happier being in the ops room and doing my bit to help other SAS operations. My shoulder does still give me the odd twinge every now and then and I still have the bullet wound scars, which I do my best to hide. I know I had made a lucky escape and other than the odd cut and bruise was the only serious wound I received during my time in the 'Regiment.'

The Australian SAS had their own firefight from hell in 2010, when on the 10 June the battle of Eastern Shah Wali Kot was raging. The large scale offensive against Taliban insurgents in the district of Shah Wali Kot, was part of ISAF's HAMKARI initiative, an ongoing civil-military activity aimed at bringing security, governance and economic opportunity to the people of Kandahar. The Australians were trying to break the Taliban's grip on the mountains, valleys and the main road between Tarin Kowt and Kandahar city. Analysts had identified the crossroads village of Chenartu of high strategic importance. Perched on a rocky outcrop and fuelled by adrenaline in the heat of the day Australian snipers lay waiting for a target. In the village below an intense barrage of machine gun fire and rockets was coming from the Taliban. Those two days in June were some of the most intense fighting the Australians have endured so far in Afghanistan. Along with the SAS was the Australian 2nd Commando Regiment's Alpha Company.

The offensive began when commandos were sent in to gather intelligence and win over locals. At dawn on 10 June, around 100 commandos were dropped in a village in order to tempt the Taliban out to fight them. In the hope Taliban commanders would order in more insurgents to reinforce them. Not long after dawn the Taliban responded and the snipers started to do their bit taking out Taliban fighters. It was a situation of kill or be killed and what would become an extremely intense firelight in searing heat. The Australian major would in between the bursts of fighting have tea with village chiefs - an important Afghan custom – before going back to join the fight as it erupted again.

The initial battle ended the same afternoon it had started when an air strike by the US destroyed the enemy on the high ground. It had been a hard day of fighting and at times, very intense. The ratio of Taliban to Commandos was about one to one. However the next day 28 Australian SAS troopers took on nearly 90 Taliban fighters in Tizak some 3 miles west from Chenartu. In Tizak the SAS had been tasked with killing or capturing a couple of Taliban commanders. It had been expected to be a routine mission – however E Troop landed in helicopters under heavy fire just after 9am.

The fire was so heavy, all they could do was crawl on their belt buckles and they could have easily have retreated. As E Troop got close to the objective, they split up to take out the machine gun positions. They were trying to get themselves dug in as best as they could under a heavy barrage of enemy fire that had virtually pinned them down. Robert-Smith then charged into a machine gun nest pinning them down killing two Taliban fighters and for that action he earned himself a Victoria Cross. Once the first machine gun position had been taken out, it turned the tide to their advantage. The SAS soldiers then systematically destroyed every machine gun position in the village, despite running low on ammunition and water, before returning to Tarin Kowt at 3am the next day. Some eighty odd Taliban fighters were left for dead out of an estimated force of around 100, with only one civilian casualty, with an elderly Afghan male who had been shot in the hand. There were no allied deaths, with only one Australian and one Afghan soldier wounded during the battle.

Chapter Nine – Suicide Bomber

Just after 2am, we were at our objective and making our way the few hundred metres to the assault point. I could hear all the radio chatter over the headsets from the various support groups - we had attached to us for this op. We made our way unhindered to the house in Kandahar and two of the troop members moved forward and peered into the house. It appeared completely quiet for a change, looking back maybe too quiet. The boss gave the order to begin the assault. We moved past a series of parked cars and then entered the house. As soon as we entered the house there was a burst of gunfire and two SAS lad's had been hit by a lone fighter lurking in the shadows of a corridor as they entered the house.

We turned round and ran back out of the door, taking the wounded with us and placed them behind one of the parked cars. The radio burst back into life with the words "CONTACT." We had taken two casualties before managing to fire a single round. Our fingers probed the two casualties for bullet wounds. I ripped open my trauma pack and helped treat the casualties. Both the wounded had been able to walk out with a little support, but with any wound it was essential to make sure they were not going to bleed to death. We needed to locate the wound and check to make sure it had not hit an important artery.

With the house now on full alert small arms fire started to rain down on the parked car we were using as cover. The skin of a car is very thin and an AK-47 can easily go straight through if the bullet does not ricochet off or stopped by a more solid element, such as an engine block. Just push the outside door panel on a car to see how thin car door panels are. Not a safe play to take over for any great length of time. There was no choice but we had to resume the assault. We approached the building under covering fire from four of the troop before Charles lobbed in a couple of grenades in quick succession.

A bit of shrapnel from one of the grenades managed to slice my finger. Adding me to the casualty list - even if it was a non-life threatening injury. Just then one of the surveillance helicopters that also had a sniper in it noticed someone come out of the rear of the house wearing a suicide vest and carrying an AK-47. The sniper got himself lined up for a shot, but the suicide bomber had found some overhead protection before he had a chance to take a shot.

Meanwhile, we were now inside the house and had already killed one Taliban fighter - as we carried out a room by room clearance. In one room we burst in, we found half a dozen terrified women cowering in the corner of the room. Once we had cleared all the rooms inside, we needed to go and clear the roof. As the leading two SAS lads got near to the top of the staircase a bomb was detonated by a suicide bomber at the top of the stairs. The blast blew them back down the stairs and on top of the rest of us. Unharmed they brushed themselves off and went straight back up shooting like men possessed. It did the trick and killed both of the final two fighters on the roof.

The suicide bomber had come out of hiding and was making his way to the car that the wounded soldiers and medic were. He did not get very far before the sniper in a Black Hawk slotted him straight through the head, before he had a chance to detonate his vest.

With all the rooms clear it was, time to gather any intelligence, even if the house was a total shambles with spent bullet casings and blood all over the place. We need to make sure we did not miss anything. We recovered, a couple of Nokia 1100 mobile phones now given the title of 'dumb phones' as all they can do is make calls and receive texts, unlike the current crop of touchscreen Smartphones that seem to be able to do just about anything.

The Nokia 1100 is the world's bestselling mobile phone with around 150 million sold. To the average UK teenager, it would be labelled a brick. In a harsh environment such as Afghanistan, its robust nature and long battery life make it ideal. I doubt an iPhone or Samsung Galaxy type handset would last more than a few days in the heat and the dust of the summer months.

Both the wounded had been stabilised and the wounds whilst serious were not life threatening. We had made a good intelligence coup with the mobile phones. The numbers and texts that may be on them would lead to other mobile phone numbers that could be traced and yield useful intelligence.

Chapter Ten – Taliban Camp

A short while before dawn, we moved out of our OP (Observation Post) that had been our home for two cold nights and days. We dropped our bergans and started to make the final trek up to the Taliban position nearly a kilometre away high up in the mountains that border with Pakistan near to Tajikstan. We still had quite a hard trek to the ridgeline up a steep incline on the side of a mountain. The views of Afghanistan from up here were breath taking - with no sign of the war raging on below. Only the odd helicopter or jet aircraft in the distance broke the silence and an F-15 jet.

We need to have attacked our objective and withdrawn back to our OP before first light. The clock was ticking as we scrambled up the rock face trying to be as quiet as possible.

When we reached the ridgeline, we got ourselves into cover behind some rocks. In the dim moonlight the shadowy figure of a Taliban fighter could be seen about 10 metres from our position – he had started to walk towards where we were taking cover. As he walked towards us he finally caught sight of us. He quickly turned and started to run back to the tent where the other Taliban fighters were holed up. Captain Wesson gave the order to attack. We charged towards the tent, as AK-47 fire could be heard, but at that point, we could not see where it was coming from. I managed to fire one round from my C8 before I got a stoppage. Captain Wesson got the first kill - as another four Taliban fighters appeared from the tent.

I worked frantically to clear my stoppage, as the Taliban fire finally became more effective and was kicking up dust and small rocks all around us.

One Taliban fighter ran straight towards us and Gunn slotted him straight through his head. The force of the impact pushed the Taliban fighter backwards before he dropped motionless onto the cold hard rock of the ridgeline. Another Taliban fighter had tried to flank us to our right and with my stoppage cleared – I fired several bullets to the chest, which stopped his advance and he dropped to his knees before falling forward. Another Taliban fighter tried to run away from the ridgeline and a couple of rounds in the back from Gunn - sent him tumbling down the mountainside.

We moved further forward before all four of us emptied an entire magazine into the tent - just in case there were any fighters left hiding in there. With the ridgeline clear of Taliban fighters we gathered up any intelligence, which included various maps and documents that may yield information about Taliban movements or plans. Although Taliban tactics were mainly gleaned from the battlefield as we saw how they planned and carried out their attacks.

It seems that Taliban fighters have stuck doggedly to the same guiding principles of guerrilla warfare honed by the Mujahideen, the forerunners of the Taliban who fought the Soviet army to a standstill in the late 1980s.

Speed, surprise, mobility and flexibility are integral factors in such 'asymmetric' campaigns; where a smaller, irregular force faces a far larger, better-armed one. History has shown that a smaller, local force will often fare better. Their favoured guerrilla methods include ambush, sabotage, roadside bombings and assassination. Often they will probe an area to see how strong the defence is and what reaction they get.

With the tent clear we pulled back, whilst I was given the task of setting up some explosives to blow the whole of the small camp, complete with RPGs and a DShK.

The DShK originally came to fruition in 1925 at the request of the Red Army. The DShK has since been modified and updated. The current version used by the Taliban dating back to 1938 and many were 'inherited' from the Russian forces during the occupation of Afghanistan.

The DShK is a gas operated, 12.7x109 mm calibre, belt fed, air cooled machine gun that fires from an open bolt and in automatic mode only. The gas piston that reloads the next round and chamber are located below the barrel; the gas piston is of the long stroke type, and is attached to the bolt carrier. The gas chamber is fitted with a gas regulator, which requires a special wrench to make adjustments.

The heavy barrel is finned for better cooling, and is fitted with a large muzzle brake. The barrel can be detached from the weapon, but it hardly can be called "quick detachable"; it is screwed into the front of the receiver, and then fixed there by the cross-bolt, which is also screwed in place.

The ammunition feed is via non-disintegrating steel belts, from the left side only. The belt feed unit was designed as an afterthought for the original magazine-fed DK machine gun, so is clamped on to the top of the receiver.

In the manual (ground and AA) applications, the gun is fitted with dual spade grips at the back of the receiver, and a dual trigger. Charging handle is also shaped as a spade grip, and is located horizontally below and between spade grips. Standard sighting equipment is an open sight adjustable for range up to 3500 and wind direction. Additional anti-aircraft sights can be installed for AA use.

The standard mount for the gun is of a universal setup, which can be used for both ground and AA roles. Designed by Kolesnikov, this mount consists of a detachable two-wheel base and three folding legs, which form the tail-boom for ground applications and are extended to form a tripod for AA applications.

Just as I was about to move, one of the Taliban fighters who was still alive, started to fire off some rounds towards me. All four of us must have opened up simultaneously and he dropped back down much quicker than he had been able to get up.

Still being very alert for any more Taliban fighters still alive, I put a couple of rounds in the head of each body I came across – just to be sure they were dead. The explosives were planted and I set the timer for 15 minutes, which would be enough for us to get off the ridgeline and into cover before the explosion lit up the now almost dawn sky.

The plan was then to go back to our OP for another two days and observe, seeing if anyone came back to the camp and how it was resupplied. These camps were set up to both observe and if they got the chance to fire at allied aircraft. Our job was to go in and eradicate them. The problem was that they were hard to find – sending aircraft in too close ran the risk of them being fired at or shot down.

The SAS setting up of an OP goes something like what is written below, and yes the term 'Zombie Apocalypse' is used, although I have yet to see a real Zombie, the closest is Trooper Harris at 4am when you have to drag him out of his sack!

Starting Out

Before going out to create an OP, certain things must be taken into consideration. First, according to the SAS, the length of the mission is always 28 days. Therefore, enough gear should be taken with each agent for them to survive that long on the mission. Four operatives should be selected as the OP team. One with good eyes and ears, a smart guy, who will be the scout and point man. Another operative who can operate a radio and is good with explosives should make the team. Two operatives who possess sniper skills and good weapons skills should round out the team.

This team of four operatives should gather their gear together. Everything they take should make them combat ready, and survival capable. Each agent should have a handgun as well as a rifle. The two sniper agents should also carry sniper rifles. Each operative should carry five loaded magazines for each weapon, as well as 200 – 400 rounds. Each agent should also have enough rations and means to gather water for 28 days. In the SAS, these packs can weigh up to 130 pounds.

The team of operatives should then form what the SAS calls a "Chinese Parliament", where the four agents determine the plan of action. It is imperative that these four operatives determine the plan themselves, and agree to it without outside input. After all, they will be the ones performing the mission. Every operatives input should be considered during this meeting and planning session. Next, it is time to begin the operation, and head towards the objective.

Insertion/Moving to OP

Once the patrol is packed and ready, they must begin moving to the OP. Almost always the team will want to move under the cover of darkness. Though some zombies have been known to smell out a human, taking away the ability to see the team moving is essential. The patrol should move slowly and deliberately towards the OP/objective. The point man should lead the way, and determines the best and most tactical route for the team. The team should cover 360 degrees while moving.

The patrol should move as silently as possible, using pre-determined hand signals to communicate along the way. Avoid speaking at all if possible, and stopping every so often to listen to the surroundings. Stay concealed, avoid creating silhouettes, and determine ERL (Emergency Rendezvous Location) along the way. This way, if things go wrong, the team knows where to meet. If the patrol has to move through camps of other survivors, it is best to not let them know about your position. If communication was established before the mission, use a code to confirm they are who they claim to be. The SAS does this by speaking a number – the answer must add up to 9, otherwise they are considered combatants. Move slowly until you are about 500 meters to the OP.

Setting up the OP/LUP

Once the patrol is about 500 meters from the OP, it is time to set up the LUP (Lying Up Position). This is a defensive position the SAS creates behind the OP to allow for eating, sleeping, and providing cover of the OP. At this point, the patrol splits up into pairs. The 2 snipers will move up to the OP while the other two create the LUP.

For the LUP, holes are dug deep enough to allow plenty of room for each operative. Though not necessary during the Zombie Apocalypse, the SAS will actually hide every ounce of dirt removed from their holes, and leave no trace of their existence behind. In fact, they even remove with them their own body waste. During the ZA, however you must still dig the hole, and use the SAS method of stuffing chicken wire with local vegetation to create a roof. Once the LUP is created, the patrol will rotate on and off who is resting, and who is in the OP observing zombie movements.

While at the OP and LUP, the proximity to the undead may be close. Therefore, the patrol must use what the SAS refers to as "Hard Routine." This means speaking in whispers only. No fires or cooking – cold rations only. Nothing that will alert the undead. From here, the team should plan to spend a month in the ground observing zombie movements and taking notes. Though the undead movements are unpredictable, numbers can be observed, as well as supplies, possible zone entry points, and more. The patrol should take notes on everything.

Evacuate

The patrol should clean up all evidence of them being there, and return to their starting location. Be careful to use a different route than the one used to arrive. Another Chinese Parliament can be held before departure, but it should be silent and swift. Again, move during the cover of night, and get back safely. Relay all the intel to the other operatives, and make a plan from there.

Chapter Eleven – Teach to Learn

Afghan National Security Forces are made up of two main forces, the Afghan National Army (ANA) and the Afghan National Police (ANP). These groups are mentored and trained by ISAF forces. Ensuring ANSF are strong enough to enforce security throughout Afghanistan is fundamental to the ISAF strategy and essential if they are to take control of Afghanistan's security when Allied forces leave.

Once of our varied roles was to undertake training of the Afghan National police, 23 SAS (Territorial Army) had initially been involved, however, it was felt they did not have the skill set necessary and was passed back to the regular 22 SAS to continue their training and mentoring.

The current Afghan National Police was established after the removal of the Taliban government in late 2001. It receives funding, training and equipment from NATO states. Various local and Federal government employees from the United States as well as Germany's Bundespolizei (BPOL), the United Kingdom's Ministry of Defence Police provided most of the training with input from the SAS.

In 2002, the EU-led mission (EUPOL Afghanistan) was heading the civilian policing in the Kabul area, but by 2005 the United States established training programs in all the provinces of Afghanistan. The Afghan National Police had nearly 149,000 active members in September 2012, which is hoped will reach about 160,000 by 2014. More recently, the Afghan government, with persuasion from NATO, has employed local police forces known as Arbakai or Afghan Local Police (ALP).

The ANP is composed of the following sub-agencies:

Afghan Uniform Police (AUP) The AUP is the primary civil law enforcement agency in Afghanistan. It is divided into five regional command centres, as well as the Afghan National Civil Order Police or

ANCOP. Other forces falling under the command and control of the ANP include local traffic police departments and the fire department.

Afghan Border Police (ABP) The ABP are responsible for securing the borders of Afghanistan against the illegal entry of persons and the smuggling of illegal goods.

Afghan Highway Police The highway police are a sub-department of the national police that is currently being dissolved. Their primary responsibility is to provide traffic safety and overall security of the 'Ring Road' highway that connects most of the major population centres in Afghanistan. Some of their roles are due to be undertaken by the new ALP.

The primary vehicle of the ANP is the four-wheel drive, diesel, 4-door Ford Ranger (and Ranger SORVs), provided by the United States in their thousands. Other vehicles include Humvees (2256 ordered in 2010), diesel-powered variants of the U.S. consumer Nissan Frontiers, Toyota Hilux pickup trucks exported from Thailand, and Volkswagen Transporter T4/Eurovans, as well as Yamaha motorcycles donated by Japan. Older vehicles, like the UAZ-469 all-terrain vehicle, were obtained from the Soviet Union.

The ANP carries a variety of weapons but has since been standardised to Smith & Wesson Sigma 9mm, AMD 65 assault rifles, AK-47 assault rifles, Vz. 58 assault rifles and rocket-propelled grenade systems.

The Uniforms worn and body armour are sometimes mismatched and poorly distributed. Most police personnel are issued with at least one uniform that is changed depending on the season when it can be either very hot or very cold. It is common to find a varying array of blue, green and grey uniforms amongst the police due to different manufacturers and the rapid growth of the force in the past few years. Some police officers have resorted to having their own uniforms custom made. Body armour is only issued as and when needed and is a mixture of Russian, Chinese and American. Plans to upgrade weapons and uniform are being drafted by the Afghan government. Typically, the ANP badge is worn on one shoulder and the Afghanistan flag on the other.

The training we gave to the ANP was mainly weapons handling and general military training including some SF training for such things as hostage rescue and dealing with larger scale attacks and terrorism. The on-going issue we had and still have - is those that defect to the Taliban and take operational knowledge with them, or those that decide to switch sides and create a green on blue situation.

Green on blue attacks is the name given to a growing series of incidents where seemingly rogue Afghan security forces turn their guns on NATO counterparts. These insider attacks have led to the deaths of more than 50 NATO troops during 2012. Subsequently, NATO responded in September 2012 by halting joint operations with Afghan security forces to prevent further attacks, following the deaths of six International Security Assistance Force (ISAF) troops in one weekend.

With the increased frequency of green on blue attacks, the topic has become an important subject for western media. It is usually portrayed as a religious and cultural problem in which Afghan troops react to perceived insults by American troops' behaviour. Others cite Taliban infiltration into Afghan security forces. However, the reasons behind these attacks go much deeper than cultural and religious incompatibilities or suspected Taliban infiltration. Rather, the motivation behind the green on blue attacks has developed over the past half a decade of NATO operations in Afghanistan. Many have grown frustrated with the occupation and the perceived treatment of Afghan's by NATO forces to local people.

Most of those rogue soldiers who undertook the green on blue attacks have become lethal enemies, usually after losing a family member through NATO airstrike's or NATO fire. If someone is killed as a result of an accidental NATO bombing or action, it is likely that they left a family behind. This will mean the family's pride is wounded and someone in the family must bring the pride back. This can lead to the need for retribution and the green on blue attacks that seem to becoming more and more prevalent.

Over the past years, most who joined the Taliban were those brothers and fathers who had lost loved ones to allied fire. One of the main reasons the allied forces are so careful with any airstrike of assault, and why the more surgical type raids provided by the SAS, especially in built up areas are preferred. Fifty standard soldiers and a few tanks will almost certainly mean civilian casualties, even if the civilians just get caught up in the crossfire. There is no real answer as in war innocent people get killed. However, by educating the local populous and showing them we are there to help them, ensuring the ANP and Afghan Army are well trained, equipped and paid properly will go some way to resolving the population. To use a standard British Army term 'winning the hearts and the minds.' This term was first used during the Malayan Emergency where practices to ensure the British kept the Malayans' trust and reduced a tendency to side with ethnic Chinese communists. The main element was to give medical and food aid to the Malays and indigenous tribes to keep them onside.

Chapter Twelve – Caving

Taking shelter under a ledge on the side of the mountain, we could hear the Taliban fighting above. A predator drone was circling high above recording the fight. Delta Force was engaged in some fierce fighting trying to get into a cave complex. We had been due to give Delta Force fire support, but they had gone in slightly too early after communication confusion and our radios falling over.

By going in earlier than expected, we had been unable to get into position and we were now pinned down. Delta was doing their best, but judging by the sound and tone of their voices things were starting to turn bad. We needed to go in and give some fire support. The predator drone feed to HQ was then relayed back to us, and helped us formulate a plan and potential route to take out the Taliban position.

Delta had already got one fatality and another minor injury, so any plan needed to be formulated and put into practice quick time. The boss was not quite his usual sharp self and it was our sergeant, who came up with a workable plan. The plan was for us to spilt into two and one team of four to flank from the right and one from the rear. Using the predator drone to gives us updates on Taliban positions and help us vector in on them.

The Predator is another great piece of kit able to undertake missions of up to 24hours. Manufactured by General Atomics MQ-1 Predator is known as an Unmanned Aerial Vehicle (UAV) and is used primarily in the USAF and Central Intelligence Agency CIA. It was initially conceived in the early 1990s initially just for reconnaissance and forward observation roles, the Predator carries cameras and other sensors, but has been modified and upgraded to carry and fire two AGM-114 Hellfire missiles or other munitions and called the MQ-1A. The final 195th Predator was delivered to the USAF in March 2011. The aircraft has been in use since 1995, and has seen combat over Afghanistan, Pakistan, Bosnia, Serbia, Iraq, Yemen, Libya, and Somalia. In total 70 Predators have been lost, 55 were lost to equipment failure, operator error, or weather. Four have been shot down in Bosnia, Kosovo, or Iraq and 11 more were lost to operational accidents on combat missions.

Notable Afghan Predator missions so far are:

During February 2002, armed Predators were used to destroy a sport utility type vehicle belonging to suspected Taliban leader Mullah Mohammed Omar and inadvertently kill Afghan scrap metal collectors near Zhawar Kili because one of them resembled Osama bin Laden.

On March 4, 2002, a CIA-operated Predator fired a Hellfire missile into a reinforced Taliban machine gun bunker that had pinned down an Army Ranger team whose CH-47 Chinook had crashed on the top of Takur Ghar Mountain in Afghanistan. Previous attempts by flights of F-15 and F-16 Fighting Falcon aircraft were unable to destroy the bunker.

On April 6, 2011, the Predator had its first friendly fire incident when observers at a remote location did not relay their doubts about the target to the operators at Creech Air Force Base.

We split up into two separate teams and began a climb that was more of a scramble up a loose rock face to get into a decent firing position. The first team came under fire almost straight away and they became pinned down. We were a little luckier and with the help of the feed from the Predator managed to go round the back of a group of Taliban fighters before opening up. That was four fighters down and what looked like another twenty to go. The other team had gone back down the rock face and tried going in from a different angle with greater success and also taking out a Taliban position of two Taliban fighters.

Delta Force was still pinned down and getting low on ammunition. Air support was available, but due to the close proximity and difficult terrain, making use of it ran the high risk of a blue on blue.

The next position the Predator had got us vectored onto had heavier weapons, including a LMG (light machine gun) in the form of a PK, 50mm mortar and RPGs. This position was the one that was causing Delta Force the biggest headache. The mortar and RPG fire and been pretty inaccurate. It was the PK that had cut down a Delta operative. The PK is a 7.62 mm general-purpose machine gun that was designed in the Soviet Union and is still in production. It was introduced in the 1960s and used by a whole host of countries around the world.

They had a good bunker position that would have taken quite a bit of effort to neutralise if we had not gone for a more direct attack. I could just about make out one of the bunkers occupants in my sights. The concern was that if we took one out, then the PK fire would start to rain down on us.

Barnes, being as mad as ever, volunteered to crawl on his belt buckle and lob in a grenade, if we put down some covering fire. Barnes started his crawl on his belt buckle. I put the butt of my rifle into my shoulder and took two short breaths and holding it, before gently pressing the trigger and letting off a shot. The shot went straight into the bunker and slotted an RPG gunner, just before he launched an RPG. As expected the PK fire turned on us and we began to fire into the bunker. The PK fire was accurate and we needed to come in and out of cover to give covering fire for Barnes. Barnes was now a mere 10 metres from the bunker and closing in fast. At about 3 metres, he pulled the pin and held the grenade for a few seconds before throwing it into the bunker. A hollow blast followed with smoke pouring out of the bunker was the end result.

Barnes stayed low made his way in and let off a few rounds to ensure everyone inside was dead. The grenade had made a bit of a mess with blood splatted inside and three Taliban Fighters lying motionless with one minus his head.

With the bunker silenced Delta Force was finally able to move forward and into the caves, killing seven Taliban fighters in the process. The other SAS team moved into a position so that they could give 'over watch' to Delta Force as they went into the caves. We held firm at the bunker – keeping eyes on for any Taliban movements towards us, although the Predator that was still flying above us had done a good enough job on its own.

With the caves and surrounding area now clear, we were ordered to move out before two F-16's came in and dropped two JDAMs each in order to destroy the cave complex and prevent it from being re-occupied. We had saved Delta Force's arse and I am sure they would be saving ours on another occasion…

Chapter Thirteen – Day of the Jackal

We had the use of two Jackals or MWMIK (pronounced EmWimmick) or Mobility Weapon-Mounted Installation Kit. The primary role of the vehicle in the British Army is reconnaissance, rapid assault and fire support roles where mobility, endurance and manoeuvrability were important.

The Jackal is quite an imposing vehicle on first sight and a distinctive shape. It has no roof to speak of but is very well armoured even the seats offer some ballistic protection. It was built and designed with Afghanistan in mind and the requirements of that theatre of operation. It drives and handles better than the WMIK if not quite as manoeuvrable. It can have a 12.7mm heavy machine gun or Heckler & Koch GMG. Then its secondary armament is a 7.62 mm general purpose machine gun. Power to propel the 6ton Jackal comes from a 5.9 litre Cummins engine producing 185bhp to give a top speed of 81mph.

The air suspension on the Jackal did a good job of soaking up the rough terrain as we made our way to our area of operations which was right on the Pakistani border. The idea was for us to harass the narcotics trade and interrupt the flow of Opium across the border. Afghanistan has been the greatest illicit opium producer in the world and is ahead of Burma (Myanmar), the "Golden Triangle", and Latin America since 1992. By November 2001, the collapse of the economy and the scarcity of other sources of revenue forced many of the country's farmers to resort back to growing opium for export. Quite allot of Opium is controlled by the Taliban who also offer above average wages for Afghans to come and help with Opium production. The revenue they earn from the Opium trade helps fund the Taliban's war effort.

We all got loaded up and kit pilled on before making our way towards the Pakistani border. We were out for seven hours and saw nothing not even a farmer. It becomes quite desolate and baron as soon as you move away from the Helmand River. The river is the reason so many villages have been built along it. The river is the lifeblood of the province and the reason it is so green, helped by the various irrigation ditches and channels that the American's further added to in the 1970's under the "Valley Project". These are the same canals and waterways that have become dangerous to navigate by allied forces. The actual Valley project left a new landscape that lent itself to armed resistance. Irrigation ditches and dense vegetation that provided ideal cover when the mujahedin fighters ambushed the Soviets (who simply cut down the trees to block the canals and lay thousands of still active mines). This led the Mujaheddin to laying their own mines, which later became IED's that they became very adept at it knowing the weak points and best places for an ambush along the canal network, information that was passed on to the Taliban. Originally, they were rebuilt from the old network of canals along the Helmand River, and new ones added. In the 1930s the Germans and Japanese reconnected 9 miles of a 200 year old stretch just before the outbreak if the Second World War. After the Second World War, the Americans came along with the Helmand Valley Project in 1946. The project was designed to irrigate 300,000 acres of desert to the west and north of Lashkar Gah and then settle 20,000 nomadic tribe people. The project lasted until 1979 and cost $136.5 million. All Americans left in August 1979 just before the Soviet invasion. The Helmand Valley project became an expensive failure, leaving a complex tribal system in place that was quite fragile and somewhat volatile. Just the Nad-e-Ali district accounted for 25 different tribal groups, making understanding local dynamics harder and 'winning the hearts and minds' almost impossible. In the 1970's various social experiments and the splitting up of tribal and ethnic groups meant that many became alienated and suspicious of authority, sowing the seeds that the Taliban would use to their advantage later on.

The Jackal has driven by our Boss, Captain Wesson – was about to stop short of what was considered a vulnerable area that contained some Russian mines. We needed to go around the minefield. Just as the Boss was about to come to a full stop there was a loud bang and the Jackal just blew up. There was a large cloud smoke and dust – bits of Jackal flew up into the air and rained down on the ground over quite a wide area. Amongst all the debris was three of the patrol, including the boss lying amongst the debris. We all looked at one another and knew what we were all thinking, "fuck no one could survive that". The Boss landed on his head 10 metres away from the explosion and got up and dusted himself looking unharmed and moving his head side to side as if to loosen it up. Johnson hit the grenade machine gun as he left the vehicle, shattering his right foot, rupturing his spleen and breaking his pelvis and back. The ballistic plate in his body armour was ripped off and propelled upwards smashing his teeth and nearly severing his tongue. Then Brown landed beside him some 30 metres in front of the Jackal. He had hit the GPMG which had sliced his left leg off just above the knee. His ballistic plate had broken his right eye socket. You really did not know where to start and who to go and give first aid to.

We all jumped out and carefully made our way towards the casualties, we had no idea if there were other mines about and decided on using the same path in and out and checking anything suspicious as we went. We needed to get a nine-liner casualty report sent as soon as possible. The Boss was clearly in shock and what he was saying made no sense whatsoever. All we could do was get everyone patched up and loaded onto our Jackal. I tried to give Brown morphine, but the Combo pen Brown had on him was broken. I then ended up administering mine to him. Once all the casualties were loaded up onto our Jackal we reversed back along our own tracks until we felt we were safely out of the minefield.

We had got an LZ set up for a CASEVAC and a Black Hawk and an Apache were already on the way to us. We got to the LZ safely and it was not long before an American Black Hawk came in and carried the casualties off, less the Boss who said he was fine and insisted he stayed with us. However, a few days later the Boss kept complaining of persistent headaches, and he took himself to the military hospital on base. With a couple of x-rays and checks the doctor found the Boss to have bleeding on the brain, and he was sent back to the UK not returning for the rest of our tour.

Both Brown and Johnson were fine if in a bad way, Johnson was out of action for 12 months, but returned to active duty with the regiment. Brown was medically discharged after losing his leg. Unable to come to terms with his life changing injury he was found six months later, sitting in his car in the garage. Brown had put a hose pipe in the car exhaust and secured it with gaffer tape. Then taken the pipe round the car and fed it through the driver's side window. Brown then committed suicide and died from carbon monoxide poisoning. He left behind a loving wife and four year old daughter. This is the other sad side of war, the war that for many has not ended and they are still fighting the demons back home be it the UK or any other country a serving soldier returns home to.

Chapter Fourteen – Ambush

We had just been alerted to a group of Taliban fighters in pickup trucks making their way into Helmand. They were connected to a recent spate of IEDs that had caused havoc with recent convoys and lives lost. This was a target too good to miss and spotted by an American drone on routine patrol. A couple of AV-8Bs came in and took one truck out and damaging another. This was a quick reaction operation and was a case of grabbing our kit, mounting our ride to quickly set up an ambush on what was left of the convoy. This was a rare opportunity to capture about 20 fighters in one go. Our task was to ensure they did not escape and the convoy destroyed. What we had not counted on was how long this ambush and subsequent contact would last.

We had around 10 minutes to get into position before the convoy appeared moving at speed. The three remaining pickups were almost shrouded in dust and hard to pick out. Due to the speed of getting into position we had no real support attachments or heavy weapons. The ensuing firefight would require our trusty C8 and a few grenades, although the close quarter firefight we ended up in, meant we never got to throw a grenade.

With the first few shots the pickups skidded to a stop and the Taliban fighters poured out. Instead of trying to find cover, they quite simply ran at us at a fearsome pace with AK-47s blazing away. The return volley of fire was intense - such was the shock and awe of this act of bravery or sheer stupidity. It caused us to find cover and be on the defensive instead of offensive. I got myself behind a wall as the rounds bounced off the wall. One of the lads was just getting into cover when an AK-47 round hit him squarely in the back, shattering the ceramic plate in his body armour. At the same time saving his life and leaving him with nothing more than a nasty bruise.

As we started to return fire the Taliban fighters started to find cover as well and in some instances were only 20-30 feet away. They fought hard and it took over an hour before we could start moving up on them. The fire remained fierce and these were highly skilled and determined fighters. It took all our skill and training to push them back. One by one we picked them off - some still continuing to fire even after they had been hit several times. We did wonder if some of them were under the influence of drugs. Either way this group of fighters were more than a worthy foe and the most tenacious and resilient group I had come across. We were lucky not to take any casualties ourselves such was the intensity and accuracy of fire. 20 Taliban fighters lay dead in a very gruesome and macabre scene, such were their injuries. Many injuries were down to the number of 5.56mm rounds needed to take them out. When you are dealing with fanatics who are determined to fight to their death the British Army policy of shoot to wound - so the enemy has to treat their wounded does not apply to the Taliban, who just carry on fighting. The lower calibre 5.56 rounds are designed to maim not kill. This is why recently the SAS top brass has taken on our debriefs, where we have reported bloody clashes with Taliban jihadists who managed to ignore their bullet wounds and carry on shooting at us. The 5.56 round is manufactured by BAE Systems in Crewe, they have a steel tip and core. The bullets are also lead-free to reduce environmental pollution. BAE has a £2 billion contract with the Ministry of Defence to produce these 'ethical rounds'.

What we require though is 7.62mm rounds along with a shoot to kill policy. The 7.62mm round will stop them in their tracks and prevent SAS soldiers being wounded or killed in the intense firefights we have all been in. There are three rifles designed for the 7.62mm round and one of these would replace the C8. We still have larger calibre GPMGs and other weapons for long range battles, but are much less effective and unwieldy in a close quarter battle that more often than not the SAS finds itself in, in Afghanistan. The rounds currently issued as standard to SAS troops for their rifles are 5.56 mm calibre. In future, the troopers will be given 7.62 mm rounds – which are almost twice as heavy and designed to kill with a single shot. The difference these bigger rounds make in a contact is akin to being able to throw a rock instead of a pebble. Potential rifles could include the US-made Special Operations Forces Combat Assault Rifle (Heavy) Mk17 – known as the SCAR-H. It is a modular rifle and fires 7.62 mm rounds from a newly designed magazine that holds 20 rounds. It can also be fitted with different length barrels for close quarter battles and be fitted with various attachments. The US Navy SEALs have been successfully using it for a couple of years and the SEAL guys we had spoken to were very impressed with it. The rifle is made by FN Herstal (Fabrique Nationale d'Herstal) located in Herstal Belgium originally founded in 1889. The MK17 Heavy comes in three versions Mk 17 CQC (Close Quarter Combat) with a 13 inch barrel, Mk 17 Standard with a 16 inch barrel and the Mk 17 LB (Long Barrel) with a 20 inch barrel. The MK17 can also be adapted to fire 5.56mm rounds with a conversion kit if the need arises. The Taliban themselves fire 7.62mm rounds from their AK-47s and Russian sniper rifles. So in effect, we are putting ourselves on an equal footing.

Chapter Fifteen - Taliban

It is important to remember in Afghanistan you are not a native of the country and even though you are there for the greater good, life in Afghanistan is far from easy. Under Taliban rule, life was even harder in Afghanistan. They ruled with an iron fist and anyone who stepped out of line was severely punished. Their belief in what they were doing was righteous and making for a better Afghanistan. Their beliefs were so strong, that one Taliban leader was bemused when the Red Cross refused to come and help him execute individuals, which he did not have the time to execute himself. Afghanistan is one of the most challenging places in the world to be a woman: More women die in pregnancy and childbirth than almost anywhere else in the world. 1 in 50 women will die during pregnancy or childbirth — one every 2 hours, 9 out 10 women are illiterate. Women have more than 5 children on average, yet 1 out 10 children die before their fifth birthday. The life expectancy of an Afghan woman is 44, one of the lowest in the world. More than 50% of Afghan girls are married or engaged by 10. Almost 60% of girls are married by 16. Nearly 80 percent of marriages in poor rural areas are either forced or arranged to men much older – sometimes in their sixties. It is at the wedding that most brides first meet the man they are to marry. Once married, they drop out of education, with many staying illiterate for the rest of their lives. Islamic extremists insist women and girls stay at home, and can only leave if they are fully covered and accompanied by a male relative. In the cities most women wear a burqa that completely covers them. The fact that girls live with their husband's extended family often results in them being treated like servants or slaves, leaving many women to feel isolated. Under the Taliban rule, women were treated worse than any other point in the history of Afghanistan. They were forbidden to work, to leave the house without a male escort, to seek medical help from a male doctor. Under the Taliban regime, women were also forced to cover themselves completely from head to toe, even covering their eyes. Women who were doctors and teachers suddenly were forced to be beggars and even prostitutes in order to feed their families. Women accused of prostitution were publicly stoned to death in the soccer stadium in Kabul.

Life in the city is different to life in a rural area. In many ways those living in the more affluent parts of the larger towns and cities have a lifestyle that is not too dissimilar to the one we live in Western Europe or North America. Years of fighting has reduced the male population greatly not just the current Afghan war, but also the previous war with the Russians. Afghanistan has 1.5 million widows, one of the highest proportions in the world. Part of this is due to war, but another element is due to marrying much older men or often die when their children are still babies.

The Taliban is best thought of as a highly religious and fanatical Islamists. They are a fundamentalist group and were in power in Afghanistan from 1996 to 2001. It was born out of the mujahideen that were trained in Pakistan, during the war with Russia. Mullah Omar started the Taliban movement with less than 50 followers, but soon grew in size and power. Pakistan's Inter-Services Intelligence (ISI) wanted to use the Taliban as a regime that would be favourable to Pakistan and helped them into power. Since the creation of the Taliban, the ISI and the Pakistani military have given financial, logistical and military support. Taliban fighters are not just made up of native Afghanistan's they come from a whole host of Western and Arab countries, led by the belief that Afghanistan is a holy war that is there to cleanse and rid the country of any western influence and corruption. Below is an account from a Taliban fighter in Afghanistan:

In any war, there is always more than one side to a story, and Griffin had once read a really interesting account of a Taliban fighter. In some ways, it almost made him feel sorry for them. They had an overwhelming feeling that theirs was a just cause and they were simply fighting for their own country. This, however, had come at a great cost with a Taliban regime that was deemed oppressive. It would happily have both soldiers and civilians killed to ensure its laws were followed and rid Afghanistan of allied forces. Still, the account that Griffin had read was quite thought-provoking and provided an insight into how the Taliban operated.

Chapter Sixteen – Hostage Rescue

I could feel the vibrations from the Chinook through the lightly padded seat, outside it was dark and dawn would be upon us in an hour. We were on a dawn raid to rescue a hostage. A Lynx helicopter was also coming along with us. The hostage was an Italian journalist had she had been snatched from a black Pajero 4x4 in Kabul a few days earlier. The Taliban had released a tape with their demands, otherwise the journalist would be killed. Intelligence had not known the exact whereabouts, but believed they had headed towards the mountains on the Afghan/Pakistan border. It was a tip off from a village nearby and a Predator drone that had found the potential hideout. No one was a 100% sure, but on watching the surveillance footage from the Predator did match the descriptions of some of the hostage takers involved.

A plan was formulated and we were bundled onto a Chinook and taken to an LZ some two miles short of where the hostage was believed to being held. The area offered good protection for an attacking force and some good areas that we could place a sniper to act as overwatch. At 4am, we were on the ground and making our way to the objective. We wanted to be in position ready to start the attack by 4.30am, so needed to get on our toes and move quickly.

I was lying down behind a bush just before 4.30 am, waiting for the snipers to let us know they were in position. Therefore, they could take any of the targets out before we pushed forward. There were two buildings, a smaller and a larger one of the normal mud construction found in Afghanistan. We hazard a guess that the hostage would be in that one and would be the main focus of our assault. We needed to make sure we got to the hostage before the hostage takers did, as they would kill the journalist in revenge for our attack.

The sniper had two targets lined up in his sights; one was a guard on the door to the smaller building. He would be the first target, but we decided to get even closer before the sniper dropped him. We moved closer to the compound and Captain Henson gave the order for the sniper to fire, the instant the round hit its target we pushed forward as quickly as possible. The noise of the sniper round had alerted the rest of the guards and they began shouting in Pashto to awaken the others to the attack, three guards were taken out in quick succession.

I went with two others straight to the building we believed to contain the hostages. The guard was lying on his side with a big hole in his head. We shoved him out of the way of the door and I got my size tens on the door. With two hard kicks, the door fell off its hinges and we moved in. The floor was covered in dirty straw and in the corner a very freighted looking white female who looked like the picture we had been given of her. She was slightly dirty, slightly dishevelled and disorientated, I had to grab her and pull her up so I could get her to come with us. We made a very quick egress away from both buildings and into cover. The fire fight was still raging on inside the larger building with some quite fierce resistance. The Taliban were not happy, that we had come to take away their prized hostage and more Taliban fighters would be on the way.

It was decided the best thing to do was for us to get going with the hostage to the RV and the rest to undertake a fighting retreat after we had put some distance between us and the rest of the patrol. Back at the compound, the sniper had managed to drop another two of the hostage takers as they try to pursue us. They managed to get a few ineffective shots off with AK-47s, these hit the trees to the far left of us, as we made off. The journalist after all she had been through was almost out pacing us as she made her bid for freedom. Her English was much better than our

Italian was and it had not taken her long to realise we were British SAS, not sure, if it was due to our foul mouth repertoire or seeing us in action that was the real giveaway.

Our fast-paced walk back to the LZ was uneventful; the same could not be said for the rest of the patrol who had about 20 Taliban in hot pursuit who had arrived in two Toyota Hilux's. Due to the terrain, the Taliban had to dismount to pursue and where possible tried to fire off the odd wildly placed RPG. The rest of the lads were getting low on ammunition. Captain Henson had called in fire support in the shape of an A10 Warthog, its 30mm Avenger cannon would make short work of the Taliban as soon as it got on station. Due to the proximity of the Taliban to the rest of the patrol and to ensure the journalist safety we would continue to the RV (Rendezvous point) and the rest of the patrol would go onto the ERV (Emergency Rendezvous Point) that was a slightly longer distance away and await extraction.

A Black Hawk helicopter would now be sent to pick us and the journalist up and get us back to Kabul and safety. Meanwhile the rest of the patrol was finally getting fire support in the form of an A10 Warthog that swooped down to about 200 feet before opening up on the advancing Taliban; with one pass over half of the Taliban fighters were now lying dead and the fire on the fleeing SAS patrol was reduced. With the advantage, the SAS dug in and returned fire to keep the rest of the Taliban fighters pinned down so the A10 could finish the rest of the Taliban off. To some the A10 may be an ugly aircraft hence the name 'Warthog' but also like the Warthog as well as being ugly is slow, low to the ground, and almost impossible to stop due its mixture of high survivability and immense fire power. Which is what makes it such an effective platform to have as fire support, being just as effective and as menacing as the Apache on the battlefield.

With the Taliban now neutralised, the patrol could get back to the ERV. I was already on the Black Hawk flying low and at speed back to Kabul for tea and medals.

A couple of other notable hostage rescues carried out by the SAS was in 2012, the SAS carried out the helicopter raid on the cave where Helen Johnston, who was working for an aid project, was being held along with three other hostages as part of a £7 million ransom. It was conducted as a joint operation with American Delta Force at 1am in the Shahr-e-Bozorg district, a large forested area near the Tajikistan border called Koh-e-Laran. SAS and Delta Force arrived by helicopter and took part in the "long march" to a cave where four aid workers (1 British, 1 Kenyan, 2 Afghan) were being held. One of the other hostages was Moragwa Oirere a Kenyan-born aid worker who had previously worked with Save the Children.

The SAS and American SF were dropped in at 1:30am by a Black Hawk helicopter and then began a five-mile trek to their objective.

The aid workers – Helen Johnston and Moragwe Oirere and two Afghan colleagues - were kidnapped on May 22, 2012. They worked for Medair, a humanitarian non-governmental organisation based near Lausanne, Switzerland.

Badakhshan the area where they were kidnapped is an impoverished and mountainous province in Afghanistan's far northeast, and while mainly quiet, there have been pockets of insurgent activity.

Helen Johnston - studied at the London School of Hygiene and Tropical Medicine, she had worked for the charity in Afghanistan.

Morgue Orr was born and educated in Kenya and subsequently worked for Save the Children in Africa, as well as other aid projects, before working in Afghanistan.

The raid came less than two weeks after the women had been seized while trekking on horseback to treat villagers suffering from malnutrition.

David Cameron had authorised the rescue attempt after military forces in Afghanistan briefed him on the planned operation. After the raid, he described the rescue effort as "extraordinarily brave" and "breath taking." He also said, "They should know if they take British citizens as hostage we do not pay ransoms, we do not trade prisoners. They can expect a swift and brutal end." The Prime Minister also added that the rescue should serve as a warning to terrorists across the world who take British citizens hostage.

SAS soldiers, assisted by other troops from ISAF's Joint Special Forces Group, which includes elements American Delta Force soldiers and Navy SEALs, as well as local Afghan security forces, were transported to the cave by helicopter and stormed into it, freeing the four hostages.

Six heavily armed hostage-takers were killed during the rescue, officials in Afghanistan said. The kidnappers, who were believed to have been a criminal group with links to insurgents in Afghanistan, had made a ransom demand in a video.

The SF entered the cave complex and came under quite intense fire but were able to overcome the intense fire and rescue all four hostages safely, no British troops were injured and a number of Taliban and hostage-takers were killed. The cave complex in itself was a challenge to storm being on multiple levels. The kidnappers also had both a height and visual advantage, being in a commanding position. By 7:30am, all the hostages had been rescued and six kidnappers lay dead. The freed hostages were then taken from the area on foot before being placed into a helicopter back to Kabul.

A statement from the Foreign Office added, "Helen and her colleagues were rescued by ISAF forces, including UK forces, in a carefully planned and coordinated operation.

"This operation was ordered by the Commander of ISAF and was authorised by the Prime Minister.

In a statement from the American General John Allen, the overall commander of the International Security Assistance Force, which includes British and American troops in Afghanistan, said: "First, I would like to thank the Afghan Ministry of the Interior and Minister Mohammadi for their tremendous support throughout this crisis.

"Second, this morning's mission, conducted by coalition forces, exemplifies our collective and unwavering commitment to defeat the Taliban.

"I'm extremely grateful to the Afghan authorities and proud of the ISAF forces that planned, rehearsed, and successfully conducted this operation.

"Thanks to them, Miss Helen Johnston, Ms Moragwe Oirere, and two co-workers will soon be re-joining their families and loved ones."

Three Afghans captured with her were released unharmed a few days later.

Another noteworthy hostage rescue mission the regiment took on that I was not involved with. Was for the daring rescue of a CIA agent facing torture by Al Qaeda fanatics. Delta Force commandos were thought at the time to not have enough battle experience for the mission behind enemy lines. The CIA agent was virtually a dead man. He only had one chance - that was the SAS do what they do best.

The four-man patrol plucked the agent from a heavily-armed house in the Taliban stronghold of Kandahar. He had been beaten and was about to be tortured for information. The SAS operatives slid down ropes from a helicopter onto the roof of the house threw in stun grenades then burst through windows. Many Al Qaeda fighters were killed or hurt during the ensuing fierce gun battle. The Taliban and Al Qaeda fighters were taken by surprise. When they returned fire, they were disorientated and it was inaccurate - meaning not one of the patrol was hit. The assault ran with three of the patrol laying down fire on the enemy in close quarter battle whilst a fourth located the prisoner and got him back to the rest of the patrol.

They then took the CIA agent out on to the roof and he was flown to safety. The SAS helicopter flew in low to avoid detection and the guards had no hint of the rescue until the SASA stormed the compound the CIA agent was being held in.

He was found after a known Taliban vehicle was tracked by a helicopter observing from a long way off through an image intensifying camera. The helicopter crew were able to pinpoint the building the CIA agent had been taken to and the Americans requested assistance for the SF. A couple of hours later the SAS went into action.'

This was a do-or-die operation in the best traditions of the SAS. There was no time or opportunity for sophisticated monitoring technology such as that used in the Iranian Embassy siege. It was a very much QBO (Quick Battle Order) style mission planned in a matter of hours.

Chapter Seventeen - Copycat

Being in the SAS, you do feel like the elite and some of the SAS operators do have a certain swagger about them. We are very good at what we do, but the fatal mistake is to think that because you are the best there is no chance of the enemy replicating what you do. The Taliban managed to do just that on an audacious raid on Camp Bastion, a raid that we would have been proud if we had carried out ourselves.

Camp Bastion is four miles long by two miles wide - built by 39 Royal Engineers. The British decided to call the new camp Bastion – a reference to the huge earth-filled bags that have been used to define its boundaries. The bomb-proof bags are made by a UK company called Hesco Bastion, which was set up by a British inventor, Jimi Heselden. He has made a small fortune selling his invention to the British military, thousands of the bags now line the roads around this camp, and almost every other in the country.

The other ubiquitous building block of the city is the shipping container, the sort you see on travelling on the backs of trains, trucks or the decks of ships at ports around the world. There are now 10,000 shipping containers at Bastion, almost all of them brought in by road through Pakistan, after being shipped from Europe or America to Karachi. There are not that many that it is estimated it could take decades to take them all away again.

Rather than bringing in water supplies from elsewhere, the British set up a water-bottling plant on site, drawing the water from the two existing boreholes. The plastic bottles are made at the plant, which provides one million litres a week for Bastion, as well as many of the other smaller bases and checkpoints across Helmand province.

Most of the fresh food is flown in, with the rest coming by road. There is a central warehouse where most of it is stored – it is said to be the second-biggest building in the whole of Afghanistan. With between 20,000 and 30,000 people on the base at any one time, the quantities needed to feed everyone are vast - 27 tonnes of salad and fruit come in every week alone. Convoys of trucks, with armoured support, thunder out of the camp most days to supply other bases, often leaving in the middle of the night to minimise the disruption to the villages and towns that they rumble through.

The base has become so big that it has eight incinerators and a burn pit to get rid of the rubbish. The camp also has its own bus service, fire station and a police force. There are on-site laws and regulations too. One of them is the speed limit – 24kph (15mph). It is enforced by officers with speed cameras, who can leap out from behind containers, or from inside ditches, to catch anyone flouting the rules. Anyone caught speeding more than three times is banned from driving on the base. Though the limit is quite low, many of the military vehicles are so big, and the dust they churn up so blinding, that it is dangerous for them to be going any faster.

There aren't any pavements at Bastion, or street lights, so walking around at night can be perilous without a torch. The airport is busy day and night. It deals with around 2,980,000 pieces of freight a month, including 73,000 pallets of mail.

There isn't much in the way of nightlife in the Camp, less the air-conditioned gyms that become regular haunts for many – there is a Pizza Hut that trades from inside a converted shipping container. Customers can even sit outside on pub-style benches. There is also a bar next door to the Pizza Hut called Heroes, which has giant TV screens showing news channels from the UK.

While the airport is the hub for flights in and out of the country, the heliport is busier. Every day, RAF Chinook, Sea King and Merlin helicopters run like buses, ferrying troops to and from the base. They are responsible for the bulk of the 600 movements undertaken across Helmand every day. There are also the Apaches that go out with them to offer top cover and also go out on a wide range of missions offering fire support to troops on the ground.

One of the most surreal sights in the city is its Afghan village, a replica built by the British Army Engineers. It has a small number of local residents who tend to a bread oven, riding motorbikes and selling food at a market. The idea of it is to give soldiers a better feel for what to expect when they go on patrol. There is also a training area designed to help identify IEDs. They have been set up so soldiers learn; they can also be taught about the different techniques for planting IEDs, and how the villagers might be trying to warn them of their whereabouts. If an Afghan has stopped using a bridge to cross a stream or a river, there is often a reason and these are the subtle points that we all pick up out on patrol.

On a dark September night just after 10pm in Camp Bastion, an explosion echoed across the Helmand desert from the east. A two-metre hole had been blasted high in the razor-wire-topped wall surrounding what was thought to be one of the most impregnable military camps on earth. Fifteen fighters dressed in American army uniforms and armed with assault rifles and rocket-propelled grenades raced through the gap.

They ran 150 metres and skirted a blast wall to run out onto a runway, bright under security lights. Alongside it were 10 canvas hangars containing Harrier jets. These Taliban attackers, a very well drilled and cohesive unit of men, divided into three teams opened fire. One group began shooting at the group of Marine Corps pilots and mechanics working on the AV-8B aircraft. The commander, Lieutenant-Colonel Christopher Raible, who always went and visited the hangars around 10pm every day, had to pull out his 9mm pistol so he could take on the attacking force

He had little chance against the intruder's superior rifle firepower and he was killed along with a mechanic, Sergeant Bradley Atwell. Nine other Marines were wounded in the attack.

The second group of Taliban fighters managed to destroy three refuelling stations. A third party then headed for the aircraft. The AV-8B Harriers had only arrived at the base in July – they have become hated by the Taliban for their deadly efficiency. Becoming just as hated as the Apache and A10. The attackers had time to plant explosives on several of the planes and others were hit with RPGs.

In total, they destroyed six aircraft and two badly damaged in the single most destructive strike on a NATO base in the Afghan war so far. It was an astonishing raid - one that David Stirling himself would have been proud of. It was reminiscent of the raids carried out in 1941 in the African desert. You could say they almost copied those audacious raids in many ways and carried this raid out to great effect.

One senior officer even said, "It was like a textbook SF attack"

As the Marines came under attack at Bastion, motion detector alarms went off in the security command post. RAF 51 Squadron, which was in charge of protection, dispatched a 15- strong force in armoured Jackal patrol vehicles

The British took an estimated 12 minutes to get to the attack after the alarm was raised and various sensors had gone off. The 12 minutes it took was simply due to the size of Camp Bastion with its 27 miles of perimeter fence.

With the 15-strong RAF squad and marines stood their ground until a further 120 NATO soldiers were in action. However, the Taliban dodged between blast walls, and their American uniforms caused confusion.

The ensuing firefight was so fierce that the RAF troops alone fired over 10,000 rounds.

The battle raged for almost four hours until a British Apache helicopter gunship ended it by finishing the Taliban off, with some 30mm cannon fire as they tried to escape across open ground. By daybreak 14 Taliban were dead and one was wounded and captured. The fear is that the Taliban has created their own special operations unit to infiltrate highly protected facilities. They suspect the masterminds to be the Haqqani network, notorious militants based in Pakistan. The Haqqanis were set up in Afghanistan in the mid-1970s and were helped by the CIA and Pakistan's Inter-Services Intelligence agency against the Soviet in the 1980s. According to US military commanders, it is "the most resilient enemy network" and one of the biggest threats to the U. S. -led NATO forces and the Afghan government.

For the raid on Camp Bastion, the Haqqani network, even had some detailed maps of Bastion as well as the correct US uniforms. That was subsequently used in the raid on Camp Bastion and led to the confusion of trying to identify who was friend and who was foe.

The Taliban must have had some form of inside information, possible information that had come from Afghan army defectors.

A local Taliban commander who gave his name as Abdul Bari told a leading Newspaper that planning began a month before the raid - when a senior Haqqani network officer asked for 20 volunteers to become suicide bombers. They were then trained in Pakistan in preparation for the raid.

The commander said an Afghan Taliban had gone to Pakistan to collect the militants a few days before the attack. They had spent two nights in a safe house in Afghanistan before striking.

The Haqqanis specialise in co-ordinated attacks and were behind the assault on the US embassy in Kabul. Despite close links with Pakistan's military intelligence, the Haqqanis have been designated as a terrorist outfit by the Obama administration.

The SAS prior to the Camp Bastian attack had helped smash a suicide bomb plot against the Afghanistan government in a midnight raid on one of their hideouts. The raid was on the same Haqqanis who led the raid on Camp Bastion, and have become dubbed "the Sopranos of the Afghan War." The Haqqanis were very close to attacking senior ministers, with a wave of suicide bombers and gunmen. The SAS helped the Afghan version of MI5 - the National Security Directorate - forced their way into the Haqqani hideout and seized four key targets in an operation just out just outside the Kabul as they prepared to launch their attack.

British SF operating helped plan the raid on a heavily protected compound in the Shur Bazaar area of Kabul City after a tip-off from local Afghans. After approaching, the area in vehicles British troops sealed off the area, allowing the Afghan NDS to storm the building, throwing stun grenades into the compound as they blasted their way in.

The Afghan NDS have worked closely with American and British SF for years on a whole host of operations and this was a textbook operation. The operation was planned quickly as the intelligence that said there was going to be a co-ordinated attack by the Haqqanis – only came a few hours before the attack was due to be carried.

The attack had the element of surprise, which meant that the NDS were able to arrest the key players. The NDS seized suicide vests, AK-47 assault rifles, rocket launchers, hand grenades, and hundreds of rounds of ammunition from the hideout. Also confiscated in the raid were a Pakistani "Identity card," along with Pakistani currency and a mobile phone.

Chapter Eighteen – Civvy Street

When the time came to leave the 'Regiment', it was more about me starting to feel burnt out as the pace and pressure of the job can be intense. The loss of Higgs had also played on my mind, and made me wonder when my luck would run out...

Leaving the SAS is much simpler than you would think. You say I am leaving, they say "OK" and then you go through the paperwork formalities hand in your kit and walk out the gate - almost within a few days. Leaving the 'lines' for the final time is quite emotional and I almost welled up inside as I passed through the gates for the final time.

Being in the Army and the SF is a lifestyle and you do get used to the camaraderie, there is a strong bond with your fellow soldiers who have experienced the same horror that you have. There is not a job in civvy street that offers the same close working relationship or the same bond and level of trust. There is an element of feeling lost on leaving the regiment even if the opportunities for a SF soldier can be quite varied. From picking up freelance work as security abroad to VIP protection and advising on a whole host of security projects. The TV and Movie industry often like ex SAS personnel to act as advisors for a whole host of new projects.

My first hurdle in leaving the regiment was to find a house, as strange as it sounded I had no need of a house and had no dependants to go home to. The world of mortgages and the process of buying a house confused and tested me more than anything I had ever done in the Army. Whilst house hunting I found my current partner who has been my rock at times and put up with my moods - as I tried to get my life together on civvy street. We are due to be married next year and she has no knowledge of my time in the SAS. To her I was just a soldier and it is better that way. I am still a target which is why our true identities are hidden and I am happy for it to stay that way. Even an ex SAS soldier can still be a terrorist target. So you have to be very careful on what we say and who we speak to especially on the military side of things.

I am just a soldier who served in the Para's, as soon as you say you are SF people start to make assumptions about you and turn you into something you are not. I'm no hero or super soldier- I am just a soldier who was lucky enough to get into the SAS and have the chance to learn skills and undertake operations that few in the world will ever know about.

For all soldiers who have served in any theatre of operation, nothing ever hides the horror of what you have seen and post-traumatic stress disorder is very real. I won't exactly say I have suffered PTSD directly, but I do have the odd nightmare and pangs of guilt for what I have seen and done. Many soldiers have committed suicide on leave or after leaving the Army over the years and that has included SAS personnel. For some, it has been the switch back to civilian life that has never fully agreed with them. For others the sense of guilt of fallen comrades, the horrific sights or even their own injury, which has pushed them over the edge.

Just after Christmas in my new job as a police officer. I was called to a job where an ex-soldier had tried to hang himself in the house, which two years previously his friend from school had hung himself. This loss of a friend that happened whilst he was away on active duty had haunted him. It was the anniversary of his friend's death and he had decided to end it all. We got there just in time as he was already hanging but still conscious and breathing. We got him to hospital and he was admitted to the mental health ward, he was then released from hospital into the care of his girlfriend 24 hours later.

Soldiers who have served and fought for their country are not always treated as the hero's they are. I am not saying I am a hero far from it, as I said I see myself as just another soldier with a job to do a job. A job that I enjoyed and kept me motivated and challenged both mentally and physically.

I could have been a mercenary or gone abroad for security work, but I had had enough of travelling and living out of a rucksack. It was nice to be settled even if the earning potential was much less. It is joining the police which has really helped me to move forward and do something different. There are the camaraderie and teamwork that I experienced in the SF, if not at quite the same level. I am able to support and be there for others in their time of need. I work with some very hardworking and dedicated police officers. It is amazing how many of my SF skills have been transferable, from greater situational awareness to intelligence gathering and investigation of crimes. I think without joining the police, I may well have gone off the rails and descended into heavy drinking, trying to find something that stimulated me in the same way as being in the SAS did.

The one element of the 'job' I do not want to ever do is be armed response, even with my background. The thought of holding a weapon again, has no appeal. Been there, done that, and had more than my fair share of chocolate medals, although a real one would have been nice!

I am lucky to have got into the police as I very nearly got myself a criminal record as a teenager. I had just finished A level classes for the day when he decided to visit a mate to see if he could pick up some cannabis. So we headed over to her place, she was this hippy chick with an apartment on a 15-story high rise on one of the top floors near the centre of Birmingham. We ended up chatting about mundane topics, we smoked a joint, and then sampled a little bit of pressed hash.

I was hovering about, when she stashed the cannabis inside of my baggy zip-up sweater and then left her apartment. It took an age for the lift to arrive. As I stood there, he heard someone's deadbolt unlatched, the door opened and this bald guy poked his head out, looked around, saw me and then shut his door. I thought it was strange at the time, but I didn't think that much of it, the lift arrived and I got on and pressed "G" for ground to head to my mums car and drive home.

As I arrived at the ground floor lobby and stepped out, I saw two uniformed Police officers standing around, with their backs to the elevators appearing to be guarding the front door. At this point, I made the quick decision to avoid a confrontation and take a right out of the lift area. So I could head out the back entrance of the building. Not long after making this decision - one of the uniformed officers turned around and saw me. As I kept walking towards the back entrance, I heard a loud, stern voice that almost made me crap myself, "Excuse me, sir!"

I turned around to see this giant of an officer, who had to of been at least 6'2" if not taller. As he walked over to be where I was standing, the cannabis was hidden inside my jumper and felt like 100+ Kg'. Not only did it feel heavy, it was also about to slip out from under my jumper. I tried to move my arm to stop it from falling, but the worst thing that could have happened...Happened. The bag rustled under my jumper and the officer looked down at where the noise was coming from. Quick thinking on my part, I knew I had to distract the officer somehow from the noise so I calmly asked.

"What can I do for ya officer?"

The officer replied in a stern voice, "You match a description we have been given. Would you mind talking to us for a minute?"

I replied in the calmest voice I could muster, "Sure."

At this point, I was thinking about how he was going to explain to my dad how their son had been arrested with a quarter pound of cannabis. I was hoping the officer would not notice my red eyes, nor the smell coming from the bag under his jumper.

The officer started again, "You match a description, could you tell me what floor and what occupant's suite you are coming from."

Now I knew something was up because he was a unique looking individual, and police officers don't just hang around in the lobby of apartment buildings questioning people who come out of the lift, so I lied and said.

"I just dropped by to visit my friend Chris on the 7th floor."

Of course, I knew no one on the seventh floor, nor did I know anyone named Chris, but the officer seemed to buy it. After a couple more questions about if he saw anyone else in the lift, the officer asked what my name was. I lied again and was both thankful and lucky the officer did not ask for any ID. After about 5-10 minutes he was satisfied that, I was not the, "suspect" they were looking for and told me to carry on my way. I knew had made a lucky escape that could have changed my life forever.

SAS troops will stay in Afghanistan to conduct counterterrorism operations against the remnants of Al Qaeda after UK combat soldiers leave in 2014.

It has been mooted that members of both the SAS and SBS will remain in Helmand Province to help Afghan forces weed out insurgents' possibly up to 2018 and beyond with SF numbers of anywhere between 10 and 200. Soldiers will continue to be lost in a war that many feel may have lost direction. All I knew is that we did our job protecting the local populous and tried to ensure as many of us as possible got home to our families.

Only history will decide how successful we were in the Afghanistan war and what the long term effects will be.

It is however worth noting that the UK Special Forces have suffered the biggest blow to fighting strength since the Second World War, with over 80 members killed or crippled in Afghanistan up until 2011. Serious injuries have left more than 70 unable to fight, while 12 have been killed. The numbers mean that by 2011 Special Forces had lost about a sixth of their full combat capacity. This is all whilst undertaking several hundred operations targeting Taliban leaders since 2007.

The death toll includes three from the SBS, one SAS officer, three SAS reservists, one member of the Special Reconnaissance Regiment (SRR), and four members of the Special Forces Support Group (SFSG). That has added to the previous toll from Iraq, where seven members of the SAS and one SBS commando died and more than 30 members of the SAS suffered crippling injuries.

The Falklands claimed the lives of 19 SAS members — 18 of them in a helicopter crash.

The pace of operations is likely to continue possibly after most of the Allied troops have left in 2014. Many of the teams have been almost continually fighting the Taliban since 2001.

Pressure on the SAS and SBS reservists to fill the gaps in manpower has continued. The high casualty rate is a result of both the scale of Special Forces operations in the past few years and the Taliban's increasing use of roadside bombs. The attrition rate has meant the operational pool has been severely depleted - largely because of the numbers of injuries. There are lots of SAS and SBS lads walking round with missing limbs. The gaps in manpower is one that needs to be addressed, but it takes a person of a certain mindset and the ability to join the SAS or SBS. One thing that will never happen is a watering down of the selection process, as that is why the UK Special Forces are still amongst the best in the world.

Chapter Nineteen – Operation Trent

During the initial phase of the war in Afghanistan, a small force of SAS and SBS were to see action in the country's deserts and mountains. The SBS would soon get themselves in one of the bloodiest and most controversial operations when they assisted in quashing a Taliban uprising at the Qala-i-janghi prison. The SAS had two full squadrons, A and G, in Afghanistan and had been deployed as part of Operation DETERMINE, which was a reconnaissance and bomb damage assessment mission. It was not the most exciting of operations for the SAS soldiers and at the time, America seemed wary of committing any ground troops, preferring to rely on air power and co-ordinate with Northern Alliance troops. Towards the end of November 2001, the SAS was given orders to attack a large opium storage facility that was also an Al-Qaeda base. It was located close to the southern border with Pakistan. Some 60-100 fanatical Al-Qaeda fighters occupied the heavily fortified base. At the time, the Americans regarded it as a low priority target; their first priority was to capture Osama bin Laden. The Americans were happy to destroy it from the air, but the British thought this may wipe out vital intelligence. The only way to capture this intelligence was with boots on the ground.

So that the SAS could co-ordinate their attack with American airstrike's, their assault was planned for mid-morning. It would be a frontal assault in broad daylight on an elevated position, without any real intelligence on the overall strength and positions of the enemy. Time was of the essence and a quick plan needed to be put in place. The plan would see Air Troop do a HALO (High Altitude Low Opening) parachute jump into the desert to secure an LZ for the six C130 aircraft to land, bringing in A and G squadron members. This would give an assault force of over 120 men and 36 vehicles, mainly WIMIKs, along with ACMAT trucks and some scout motorcycles. The SAS soldiers would then use the vehicles to drive to their designated FUP (Forming-Up Point). G Squadron was tasked with setting up a fire support base by 11am and engaging enemy positions from a standoff point. American aircraft would then destroy the opium storage.

Making use of the airstrike's and fire support from G Squadron, A Squadron would assault the opium base and do a sweep for any useful intelligence. The night before the C-130s were due to land, Air Troop performed their first operational HALO jump consisting of an eight-man team jumping off the ramp of a C-130. Once landed, Air Troop studied the ground to make sure it could carry the weight of a C-130 before they marked out a landing strip. As the C-130s came into land in the dark, Air Troop used infra-red torches to denote the landing zone

As the C-130s rolled to a stop, enveloped in the cloud of dust whipped up by their four large propellers, the rear ramp lowered and the WMIKs sped out and into an all-round defensive position. 30 minutes later, the C-130s had taken off to collect the rest of the SAS force. Once the entire force was at the LZ, the ACMAT trucks were piled high with supplies including fuel, water and ammo. The motorbikes went off first to scout for any enemy positions, as well as checking the routes the rest of the SAS convoy would travel. Under the cover of darkness, the largest wartime SAS force moved off to its LUP (Laying-Up Position) before moving out to commence the attack. The drive was thankfully uneventful, although one WMIK was lost after engine failure and abandoned where it had failed.

From the LUP, the force would move into their various FUPs before commencing the attack, although as they moved up towards the small group of buildings at the bottom of the mountainside, which was their objective, the Al-Qaeda defenders spotted the dust clouds being kicked up by their vehicles and started firing off RPGs with little success. The WMIKs lined up and started to rain down heavy fire from their 12.7 mm heavy machine guns and 7.62 mm GPMG.

A Squadron then began to push forward, driving as close as possible before jumping off the WMIKs and moving forward. They used a technique called 'pepper potting,' which is one of the basic infantry maneuverers taught to all British army recruits. The movement consists of a soldier getting up and moving forward whilst another is in the prone position giving covering fire, before the soldier moving forward goes firm. The soldier giving covering fire then gets up and moves past the soldier who has just gone firm and so on. In this case A Squadron moved up, with two giving covering fire whist two pushed forward. The fire coming from Al-Qaeda was quite intense and whilst not very accurate, Al-Qaeda was fierce and almost seemed to be enjoying the fire fight. The fire support continued to rain down and snipers were also now in position, armed with L82A1 Barret rifles, and took pot shots at various Al-Qaeda fighters. The snipers accounted for many of the Al-Qaeda fighters killed. While all this was going on, US Navy F/A18 Hornets were on station and began to fire Maverick missiles on the opium storage containers. The missiles destroyed some £50,000,000 ($78,520,000) worth of stored opium. The F/A18s also strafed various enemy positions that were pinning down the advancing SAS, narrowly missing the advancing SAS soldiers on one strafing run, which could have led to a blue-on-blue incident.

The SAS made slow but sure progress as every inch was a hard-fought one, such was the strength of the response from the Al-Qaeda fighters. As A Squadron got closer to the objective, they started to take casualties, one of which was serious. Rounds were dancing round their feet and ricocheting off the rocks around them. A Squadron finally made it to the main base and made their way through, clearing buildings and checking the HQ building for any useful intelligence. The battle had raged for four hours and the base was now littered with Al-Qaeda corpses.

The Regiment had taken relatively light casualties. Even though the base appeared clear, the SAS still had to undertake a tactical withdrawal just in case they came under renewed effective enemy fire. The four SAS casualties were evacuated by a US Chinook and the rest of the SAS returned to their LZ to be recovered by the same C-130s that had dropped them off.

This story along with sixteen other Special Forces stories from around the world, can be found in Steve Stone's **Black Ops: Heroic Tales**

Other books by Steve Stone:

ISIS Dawn – The Special Forces battle against ISIS in Syria and Iraq.

Delta Force: Tango Uniform – Follow Delta Force in the 1991 Gulf War searching for SCUDs

Black Ops – 32 explosive Special Forces stories from around the world.

Stirling Work - The true story of the original SAS during WWII.

Glossary

AK-47 – The AK-47 Kalashnikov assault rifle more commonly known as the AK-47 or just AK (Avtomat Kalashnikova – 47, which translates to the Kalashnikov automatic rifle, model 1947), and its derivatives. It had been and still is with minor modifications, manufactured in dozens of countries, and has been used in hundreds of countries and conflicts since its introduction. The total number of the AK-type rifles made worldwide during the last 60 years is estimated at 90+ million. The AK-47 is known for its simplicity of operation, ruggedness and maintenance, and unsurpassed reliability even in the most inhospitable of conditions.

Apache AH64 – The Bowing Apache AH64 is a twin engine attack helicopter with quite formidable firepower consisting of a fully movable 30mm cannon, rockets and Hellfire missiles stored in pods on the stubby wings.

AV8B – The AV8B was manufactured under licence by McDonnell Douglas and based on the Hawker Sidney Harrier jump jet. Capable of vertical or short takeoff and landing (V/STOL), the aircraft was designed in the late 1970s as an Anglo-American development of the British Hawker Siddeley Harrier. It first flew in 1978 and is powered by a single Rolls-Royce F402-RR-408 (Mk 107) vectored-thrust turbofan.

C8 - The C8 was born out of the C7 when in 1984; Canada adopted a new 5.56 mm assault rifle. The C7 itself was based on a later version of the M16. To avoid research and design expenses, the Canadians simply purchased the license from USA for a new assault rifle, chambered for the latest 5.56 x 45 NATO ammunition. This was the Colt model 715, also known as the M16A1E1 rifle. Adopted as the C7, this rifle combined features from both earlier M16A1 rifles and the newest M16A2. Later on,

Diemaco (now Colt Canada) developed a short-barrelled carbine version, fitted with telescoped buttstock, which was designated the C8.

CH-47 Chinook - The CH-47 Chinook is an American helicopter built by Boeing with a tandem rotor design. It first flew in September 1961 and has gone through many changes since then. Originally powered by two Lycoming T55-GA-714A turboshaft engines. It has seen service around the world with the USAF, USMC, RAF in a variety of conflicts and wars. It is currently in service with 26 different countries and a total of 1179 have been built. The SAS uses a specially adapted 'Special Forces' version of the Chinook. Eight Chinook HC3s were ordered in 1995 as dedicated special forces helicopters, which were intended to be low-cost variants of the US Army's MH-47E. The HC3s include improved range, night vision sensors and navigation capability.

DShK – The DShK is a Russian heavy machine gun that came into service in 1938. It is gas operated, with a 12.7x109 mm calibre belt fed and air cooled machine gun. It can be used as an anti-aircraft gun mounted on a pintle. It is also easily mounted to trucks or other vehicles as an infantry heavy support weapon.

General Dynamics F-16 'Fighting Falcon' – The F-16 is a single engine supersonic, multirole fighter aircraft, developed for the USAF. It first flew in January 1974 and is powered by a single F110-GE-100 afterburning turbofan engine. It is one of the most manoeuvrable aircraft in the world and is used by the U.S. Air Force Thunderbirds display team and has been exported to quite a few air forces around the world.

Heckler & Koch 417 - The Heckler & Koch HK417 is a rifle manufactured by the German manufacturer Heckler & Koch. It is a gas-operated, selective fire rifle with a rotating bolt and is basically an enlarged HK416 assault rifle. Chambered for the full power 7.62x51mm NATO round, instead of a less powerful intermediate cartridge, the HK417 is intended for use as a designated marksman rifle, and in other roles where the greater penetrative power and range of the 7.62x51mm NATO round are required. It has been adopted for service across the world by armed forces, Special Forces, and police organizations.

Heckler & Koch MP7 - The Heckler & Koch MP7 is Personal Defence Weapon manufactured by the German manufacturer Heckler & Koch. It is chambered for the HK 4.6×30mm cartridge. It was originally designed with the new cartridge to meet NATO requirements published in 1989, as these requirements called for a personal defence weapon (PDW) class firearm, with a greater ability to defeat body armour. The MP7 went into production in 2001.

Humvee – The HMMWV (High Mobility Multipurpose Wheeled Vehicle), commonly known as the Humvee, is an American four-wheel drive military vehicle produced by AM General. It has largely supplanted the roles formerly served by smaller Jeeps. It has been in service since 1984 and served in all theatres of war. Powered by an 8 Cylinder. Diesel 6.2 L or 6.5 L V8 turbo diesel and with a top speed of over 70 mph, which drops to 55mph when loaded up to its gross weight. It initially lacked any armour but later version has had some armour protection added against small arms fire.

Lockheed C130 Hercules – The Lockheed C130 Hercules is a four engine turboprop transport aircraft with a high wing design. It first flew in August 1954. Since then there have been many variants used by over 70 countries around the world. Originally powered by four 4 Allison T56-A-15 turboprops. It can carry a payload of around 20,000 kg or up to 92 passengers. It is a highly versatile aircraft and has seen use across the world over its 50 years of continuous service.

M1 Abrahams Tank – The M1 Abrahams main battle tank is a notable tank. One of its more unique features is the fitting of a Honeywell AGT1500C multi-fuel turbine engine. Where most of its contemporaries have used diesel engines. It entered service in 1980, replacing the M60 main battle tank. It has received several upgrades to its weapons systems and armour since introduction. It has a top speed of 42mph on the road and 25mph off road.

M4 Carbine - The M4 carbine is a family of firearms that are originally based on earlier carbine versions of the M16 rifle. The M4 is a shorter and lighter variant of the M16A2 assault rifle, allowing its user to better operate in close quarters combat. It has 80% parts commonality with the M16A2. It is a gas-operated, magazine-fed, selective fire, shoulder-fired weapon with a telescoping stock. Like the rest of the M16 family, it fires the standard .223 calibre, or 5.56mm NATO round.

M16 – The M16 is a lightweight, 5.56 mm, air-cooled, gas-operated, magazine-fed assault rifle, with a rotating bolt, actuated by direct impingement gas operation. The rifle is made of steel, 7075 aluminium alloy, composite plastics and polymer materials. It was developed from the AR-15 and came into service in 1963. The M16 is now the most commonly manufactured 5.56x45 mm rifle in the world. Currently the M16 is in service with more than 80 countries worldwide. It has grown a reputation for ruggedness and reliability and was adopted by the SAS over the less reliable SA80. Later the SAS adopted the C8.

McDonnell Douglas F15E 'Strike Eagle' – The F15E Strike Eagle is an all-weather multirole fighter, derived from the McDonnell Douglas (now Boeing) F-15 Eagle. It is powered by two Pratt & Whitney F100-229 afterburning turbofans, 29,000 lbf and capable of Mach 2.5 (2.5 the speed of sound). It first flew in December 1986 and an F15SG version is on order by the ordered by the Republic of Singapore Air Force (RSAF).

Northern Alliance - The Afghan Northern Alliance, officially known as the United Islamic Front for the Salvation of Afghanistan, was a military front that came to formation in late 1996 after the Islamic Emirate of Afghanistan (Taliban) took over Kabul. The United Front was assembled by key leaders of the Islamic State of Afghanistan, particularly president in exile Burhanuddin Rabbani and former Defence Minister Ahmad Shah Massoud.

General Atomics MQ-1 Predator – The Predator is a UAV (Unmanned Vehicle) used for reconnaissance of targets and the for battlefield observation. It first flew in July 1994 and powered by a single Rotax 914F turbocharged four-cylinder engine powering a single rear mounted propeller. The MQ-1A has been adapted to carry two AGM-114 Hellfire ATGM or AIM-92 Stinger missiles.

Puma - The Eurocopter AS332 Super Puma is a four-bladed, twin-engine, medium-size utility helicopter marketed for both civil and military use. Originally designed and built by Aérospatiale, it is an enlarged and re-engined version of the original SA330 Puma. The SA330 first flew in 1965 and the AS332 in 1978. The AS332 is powered by two Turbomeca Makila 1A1 turboshaft, that each give out 1,300 kW (1,742 shp).

SIG Sauer GmbH is the German subsidiary of Switzerland-based manufacturing firm L&O Holding, which also owns Swiss Arms AG. Initially SIG Sauer Inc was established in 1985 with the name Sigarms (until October 2007) to import and distribute SIG firearms into the United States.

Sikorsky UH-60 Black Hawk – The UH-60 Black Hawk has been cemented in history after the books and film 'Black hawk down'. It is a four bladed twin engine medium lift helicopter designed for the United States Army. It first flew in October 1974 and has been used in a variety of roles and variants since then. Powered by two General Electric T700-GE-701C turboshaft engines it can carry a variety of payloads and be adapted to suit a wide variety of missions. It was designed from the outset to a high survivability on the battlefield. First being used in combat during the invasion of Grenada in 1983.

Toyota Hilux – The Toyota Hilux is a small pickup truck manufacture by Toyota in Japan. It has been produced since 1968 and is currently on its 7th generation. It can have either front wheel drive or four wheel drive. The Hilux has gained a reputation for exceptional sturdiness and reliability, even during sustained heavy use and/or abuse, and is often referred to as "The Indestructible Truck".

Warrior Tank – The Warrior tank is lightweight tracked vehicle introduced in 1988. It is powered by a Perkins V-8 Condor Diesel engine and a top speed of 46 mph. Armament consists of a 30 mm L21A1 RARDEN cannon although the 40 mm CTA International CT40 cannon is planned as a future upgrade. Secondary weapons are a L94A1 coaxial 7.62 mm chain gun and a 7.62 mm machine gun. The plan is to upgrade the warrior tanks further to keep them in service until 2025.

Westland Lynx – The Lynx is a British multi-purpose military helicopter that has been in service since 1978 and had its first flight in March 1971. It was the first aerobatic helicopter and still holds the helicopter speed record after being specially modified. Powered by two 2 × Rolls-Royce Gem turboshaft engines, the Lynx has proven itself as a versatile helicopter and quite potent as an attack helicopter. The latest version the Wildcat is due to enter operational service in 2014.

WMIK – Based on a Land Rover Defender, the WMIK was manufactured jointly by Land Rover and Ricardo Vehicle Engineering, featured a strengthened chassis and are stripped down before being fitted with roll cages and weapon mounts. Typically the vehicles can carry one 12.7 mm Heavy Machine Gun, 7.62 mm General Purpose Machine Gun (GPMG) or on occasion the MILAN ATGM, on the rear ring-mount, with an additional pintle mounted GPMG on the front passenger side. In 2007, they were fitted with a new belt-fed Automatic Lightweight Grenade Launchers (ALGL) made by Heckler and Koch (HK GMG).

ZSU-23-2 – The ZU-23-2 "Sergey" is a Soviet towed 23 mm anti-aircraft twin-barrelled autocannon. It was designed to engage low-flying targets at a range of 2.5 km as well as armoured vehicles at a range of 2 km and for direct defence of troops and strategic locations against air assault usually conducted by helicopters and low-flying airplanes. Normally, once each barrel has fired 100 rounds it becomes too hot and is therefore replaced with a spare barrel.

Bibliography

Andy Mcnab Bravo Two *Zero* (Bantam press 1994)

Barry Davis *Heroes Of The SAS: True Stories of The British Army's Elite Special Forces Regiment* (Virgin Books; New Ed edition 2007)

Chris Ryan *The One That Got Away* (Red Fox; Junior Ed edition 2010)

Damien Lewis *Bloody Heros* (Arrow; New Ed edition 2007)

Damien Lewis *Zero Six Bravo: 60 Special Forces. 100,000 Enemy. The Explosive True Story* (Quercus 2013)

John parker *SBS: The Inside Story of the Special Boat Service* (Headline; 2nd Revised edition edition 2004)

Mark Nicol *Ultimate Risk* (Macmillan 2003)

Mark Urban *Task Force Black* (Abacus 2010)

Micahel Ahser *The Regiment: The Real Story of the SAS* (Penguin 2008)

Peter Scholey *The Joker: 20 Years Inside the SAS* (Andre Deutsch Ltd; New edition edition 2007)

Peter Winner *Soldier 'I': the Story of an SAS Hero: From Mirbat to the Iranian Embassy Siege and Beyond* (Osprey Publishing 2010)

Internet

www.USNavySEALs.Com

Printed in Great Britain
by Amazon.co.uk, Ltd.,
Marston Gate.